Outside Edge

A play by

Richard Harris

Samuel French - London
New York - Toronto - Hollywood

OUTSIDE EDGE

First presented at the Hampstead Theatre, London on the 24th July 1979, and by Eddie Kulukundis at the Queen's Theatre, London, on the 11th September 1979, with the following cast of characters:

Miriam	Julia McKenzie
Roger	Richard Kane
Bob	John Kane
Dennis	Julian Curry
Maggie	Maureen Lipman
Kevin	Ian Trigger
Ginnie	Susan Carpenter
Alex	Martin Wimbush
Sharon	Natalie Forbes

The play directed by ROBIN LEFEVRE

Setting by Grant Hicks

The action takes place in a cricket pavilion

Act I A summer's day. About 1 p.m.
Act II About 5.30 p.m.

Time—the present

ACT I

A Cricket Pavilion. About 1 p.m. on a fine summer's day

The pavilion is a wooden structure, nothing grand, in need of a coat of paint. There is a drinks bar with a wooden shutter, rolled down, and a counter from which teas are served. Behind the counter is an opening to the unseen kitchen. Two high stools are at the counter. In front of the bar a folded trestle table leans against the wall. Between the bar and the counter is an elderly piano on which stands the odd cricket trophy. On the wall by the bar is a clock, and on the other side a pay phone. Above this is a notice-board, and next to it a door leading through to the changing-rooms. On another wall is a dart-board with darts, and below it some folded wooden chairs. Steps lead down from a somewhat vandalized verandah to the grass area below. On each side of the steps are wooden benches, and on the front wall to one side is the scoreboard. On one bench is a bucket of whitewash, a splattered marking-up stick and an old pair of whitewash-splattered wicket-keeping gloves. Beyond the wall with the scoreboard a wooden door leads off to the car-park. Beside this door is an upstand water-pipe with hose attached. The hose extends off towards the pitch (See plan on p. 75)

When the CURTAIN *rises the stage is empty for a moment and then Roger enters from the changing-rooms, looking at the team list which he pins up on the board. Roger is a rather pale, shortish, stocky man in his late thirties. Although very boyish, his voice is surprisingly deep and resonant. He's rather inclined to address people much like the young subaltern addressing the troops. He wears khaki shorts with bulging pockets, a white shirt and sandals with rolled-down socks. A folded daily newspaper sticks out of his back pocket*

Having pinned up the notice, he checks his watch and then moves over to put the clock forward five minutes or so. He pulls a piece of paper from his shirt pocket—this is his "list". He exits towards the pitch cheerfully, shoving the list back into his pocket

After a moment, Miriam enters from the car park. She is loaded down with two cardboard boxes containing groceries, loaves, etc., and backs on, having pushed open the swing gate with her behind. Miriam is about thirty-five. She has a good face and figure but does nothing to glamorize herself. No make-up, hair pulled back in a bandeau. A simple summer frock, not new. To all appearances, a somewhat daunting air of efficiency. She is, in fact, incredibly shy. She lugs the boxes straight through and exits into the kitchen, humming cheerfully

Roger enters from the pitch, turns off the water tap. He pulls out his list, frowns down at it, then becomes aware of Miriam's humming

Roger (*calling*) Miriam!
Miriam (*off*) Here I am darling, don't panic.

Roger moves inside

Miriam enters and takes a cardboard box of crockery from beneath the counter and puts it on top

Roger You know it isn't on. It just isn't flippingwell on.

Miriam (*busying herself*) What isn't?

Roger What? Oh—thingy—wassisname—Alex.

Miriam He hasn't let you down again, has he Roger. I don't know, it's so unfair.

Roger Touch wood, of course he's playing—don't say things like that, Miriam, please—I'm scraping the barrel as it is. (*Looking at his list*) Cups, broken, three.

Miriam (*pointing into the box*) Cups, replaced, three.

Roger When?

Miriam I told you—this morning.

Roger Sorry. Couldn't have. (*He points*) It's on my list.

Miriam Sorry darling—twice. Once when I woke you with your grapefruit and the weather forecast and once when I was driving you here. Sorry darling.

Miriam beams brightly at him and goes into the kitchen

Roger You don't half mess me about at times, Mim, I don't make out this list for fun, it is all down to me you know, all this. (*He pulls out a stub of pencil and crosses out "cups" from his list*)

Miriam enters from the kitchen with a tea towel

Miriam What about Alex?

Roger Mm? Oh—he volunteered to help me roll the pitch. One o'clock, promise. I don't know why I bother at times, really I don't. (*He pulls the paper from his pocket and moves to sit on the steps to read from it*)

Miriam comes out from behind the counter, goes to the piano, lifts the lid, takes out a key hidden there, moves to unlock the bar door and puts her head inside momentarily checking

(*During this*) The point I'm trying to make is that they've got no right saying they'll be here if they've got no intention of being here. I'm here, why can't they be here?

Miriam Tell them.

Roger (*reading*) The dry weather is expected to continue.

Miriam I've told you the forecast.

Roger Temperatures will reach around twenty degrees centigrade, falling to twelve degrees overnight.

Miriam You're always going on about making a stand at the wicket; all right, make a stand in here. Tell them.

Roger Winds fresh to strong, dying away by mid-afternoon.

Miriam Why should everything be left to you? It's so unfair.

Roger Further outlook continuing dry with perhaps the chance of rain later tomorrow.

*Pleased, Roger gets up and puts the paper down on the bar counter. Miriam
returns to busy herself behind the tea counter*

Mim—if I start laying down the law, half of them won't turn up at all. All
I can do is what I do now; ask for volunteers. And they do, let's face it,
they do volunteer.

Miriam It's just that they never show up. (*With her sudden overbright smile*)
But I show up, don't I, darling? Every week, I show up.

Roger Ah yes! But then—you're the captain's wife.

Miriam Oh I see.

Roger Fair do's, Mim. (*He mimes a forward defensive stroke*) I love you. Okay,
fair enough?

Miriam And I love you.

*He moves to the counter and leans across it and she leans across from behind
it and they mime a rather chaste little kiss with their faces not actually touching.
He soon moves away again*

Roger The truth is, if you weren't here, it just wouldn't be the same. Couldn't
be. And you know why, don't you?

*She takes up a rubbish bin and moves out to pick up the odd piece of rubbish
from the verandah and grass*

Miriam We're very lucky: we like being together.

Roger There's that, yes—(*he stares out over the pitch*)—but not only that,
Mim. Teams *want* to come here and play us, you know, Mim—not only
because of the game, but because of your teas. Your teas are talked about
throughout the entire South Western League, d'you know that?

Miriam Not the *entire* South Western League, surely?

Roger Cross my heart. As for my side of things—all right, okay, fair enough—
maybe I do take on more than my fair share, maybe I should get more help—
but we're not talking about chaps at school you know Mim, we're talking
about grown men pretty much set in their ways. I start laying down the
law about fatigue duties and I destroy everything I've built up over the past
two years. What's twenty degrees centigrade in whatsit?

Miriam Umm ...

Roger I mean, crumbs Mim, last year we didn't even have this place and now
I'm really getting my feet under the table, there's no knowing where it could
lead to: premier league, winter tours, who knows? Sometimes I lie awake
at night, just thinking about it.

Miriam So do I.

Roger It's a team, Mim. A fighting unit if you like and I'm the captain.

*Miriam moves inside and behind the tea counter as he continues, staring out
over the arena*

It's me who controls whether we win or lose and I want to win, Mim, no
point else. There's this very fine balance. It's all psychology, which means
tact and diplomacy and ... (*Suddenly he clicks his fingers at her as he remembers*) Thingy, whatsit, notice.

Miriam Please don't do that, Roger, you know I don't like it. (*She dutifully reaches under the counter to produce a white cardboard sign*)

Roger takes it. It reads "Ladies First Door on Right". He hangs it on a hook on the changing-rooms door

Roger Right. I'll get on with the marking up. (*He snaps his fingers at her*) What's next from your side of things? (*He moves outside*)

Miriam Toilet requisites—and do say something about them stealing the soap Roger, *please.*

Roger pulls on the white-splattered gloves from the bench

And it's sixty-nine.

Roger (*frowning*) What?

Miriam Degrees Fahrenheit.

Roger Super!

Roger takes up the bucket and stick and exits cheerfully in the direction of the wicket. Miriam takes a box into the kitchen, reappears moments later with two bars of soap, a double roll of Andrex and an aerosol spray and exits, humming "I can give you the starlight", into the changing-rooms

Bob *enters from the car-park, looking decidedly furtive. He looks towards the wicket as he hurries into the pavilion, glances around to make sure no-one is there, moves quickly to the phone, and dials, bending low to read the numbers. Bob is in his late thirties. A slim, restless man who smokes far too much, bites his nails and is generally guilt-ridden. Wherever he is, he feels he shouldn't be. He wears glasses and casual clothing which though not new was expensive originally.*

As he waits for the phone to be answered he lights a cigarette with lighter. Eventually he presses in his two pence

Bob (*brightly*) It's me, hi ... At the club—you know— cricket ... You know me, never give up. Anyway, you phoned ... Sorry? ... No, not really, she was in the bedroom drying her hair, but maybe it isn't such a good idea to phone me, not at home, not for a while anyway, you know what she's like ... Sorry? ... No of course you don't know what she's like, I mean *I* know what she's like and she gets a bit upset obviously. Well, she is my wife after all. (*His face clouds*) I can't come round this afternoon, why, what's happened ...?

Miriam enters through the changing-rooms door, flitting with the spray

Bob presses himself against the wall, unnecessarily cupping the receiver and giving Miriam a wave. She smiles, mouthing "Sorry", and continues her way across to the tea counter, pausing to spray into the bar

(*"Quietly"*) What d'you mean, face to face, why can't you ... no, I am not losing my temper, I'm ...

Bob turns to look at Miriam behind the counter and grins hugely and she mouths, pointing to herself, "Would you prefer me to go out?" He shakes his hand and grins wildly that she should think such a thing necessary

Miriam, anyway, goes into the kitchen

(*Back to the phone*) No of course I don't mind you ... It's just that ... Pardon? ... No I am not trying to start an argument I'm supposed to be playing cricket. I've told Ginnie I'm playing, I've told Roger I'm playing, if I turn round now and say I can't play, what excuse can I give? ... No of course the game isn't more important than ... Half-past two.

Roger (*off, calling*) Miriam!

Bob Hang on ...

Bob hurries into the changing-rooms, closing the door so that the cord is stretched across from the phone inside the door. Roger returns with the bucket, puts it on the bench and moves inside the pavilion, holding the splattered gloves up in front of himself like a surgeon. Miriam comes out of the kitchen

Roger Didn't I see Bob come in here just now?

Miriam I think you'll find him on the other end of that piece of wire.

Roger turns to look as Miriam moves out from behind the counter

I'll see you later.

Roger (*in near panic*) What d'you mean, where're you going?

Miriam I shan't be long, I'm going to the greengrocer's.

Roger Why?

Miriam Because you were going and somehow I don't think you'll get round to it.

Roger I mean why can't someone else go?

Miriam Because there's no-one else here, is there?

Roger There's him.

Miriam You'll need him. (*Searching her handbag*) Did you take the keys?

Roger No.

Miriam Are you sure?

Roger Don't patronize me, Miriam.

Miriam (*moving behind him and patting both his pockets*) I'm not patronizing you, darling, I'm looking for the car keys—and, oh, listen I think I've found them.

She delves into his pockets to sort out keys and money as he stares irritably at the messy gloved hands he holds before him

Roger What about thingy, Shirley, she could do it.

Miriam Shirley isn't coming, they're looking at houses.

Roger Then Whatsit could have done it, good God, it's on his way.

Miriam Then you should have *asked* him, shouldn't you darling? (*For the first time, she shows a slight flash of irritation and digs deeper into his pockets*)

Roger (*wincing*) But I need you here, Miriam. I mean—what if something turns up?

He wriggles away from her, crossing his legs, and she digs deeper into the pockets

Miriam Will you please—keep—still ...

Bob comes out of the changing rooms and sees them, and—pleased at the chance of a diversion—deliberately pretends to misconstrue, with a big grin

Bob Hello hello hello, go out and come in again, shall I?

Bob replaces the receiver as Miriam extracts her hands—one holding the keys, the other holding some coins and screwed-up banknotes. She takes two pound notes and the loose change and shoves the rest back in the pocket

Miriam Roger's being difficult again.

Roger I am never difficult. Bob, am I difficult?

Bob I heard you were a bit of a pushover myself. What's it all about?

Miriam (*with bright smile*) How d'you mean, a bit of a pushover?

Bob (*grinning, winking*) Ask him.

Miriam (*even more brightly*) Do I *have* to ask you, Roger?

Roger (*waving her away*) Off you go then, woman, chop chop.

Miriam (*posivitely beaming*) Please don't do that, Roger you know how it upsets me.

Roger (*clapping his hands*) Go on, go on, off you go ...

Miriam I'm going, darling, I'm going ... (*She smiles at Bob and moves quickly outside, only now showing a little of her frustration*)

Roger scuttles across to beckon her

Roger Mim ... love you.

Miriam Love you too, darling.

Bob sneaks a quick look at his watch

Miriam exits round the side of the pavilion by the car-park

Roger returns to Bob

Bob Bloody good woman you've got there, Rog.

Roger What!

Bob Bloody gem.

Roger looks around the room vaguely, trying to remember what he is supposed to be doing

Roger Mind you ...

Bob What?

Roger Sorry?

Bob Mim ...

Roger Not half ...

Bob Don't seem to have the knack m'self.

Roger Luck of the draw, if you ask me.

Bob (*suddenly depressed*) What a mess I've made of my life. And it's not just my life, is it?

Roger You know what *I* think, Bob?

Bob No?

Roger I think we should get this table up. (*He moves to stare down at the trestle table, leaning against the rear wall*)

Bob Right! Where d'you want it?

Roger continues to stare at the table

Roger That's a point. Tell you what. Best wait till Mim gets back, we'd only be messing up her system. (*Totally decisive*) Leave it. (*He does his finger-snapping-pointing bit*) Roller.
Bob I thought it was Alex's turn this week?
Roger Swore blind, and where is he?
Bob He always swears blind.
Roger (*slapping his hands together*) All set, then?
Bob Well I would, Rog, only I've got a bit of trouble. I mean, I would, you know I would.
Roger What d'you mean, trouble? Don't say it's your bloody back again, I've got you down at number three. (*He goes to stare at the team list as if to prove the point*) Look, there you are, in writing. B. Wiley, number three.

Bob moves to stand next to him, staring at the list, lighting another cigarette

Bob Oh well. Now then. I'm not keen on that, Rog, not number three. You know me, four or five topweight.
Roger If I had to put my life on a man going in at number three and making a job of it, you know who that man would be, don't you?
Bob Coupla years ago maybe.
Roger *Now.* You are all right are you, I mean, your back?
Bob Oh yes, no trouble there, Rog, I feel in really good nick, you know what I mean? Really good nick. (*He flexes his shoulders to prove the point*)
Roger Super.
Bob (*staring at the list again*) And you really want me in at number three.
Roger I really want you in at number three. (*He claps a gloved hand on Bob's back*) You being the only genuine all-rounder in the side.
Bob (*sighing*) Yeah.

Bob turns and moves away, and Roger sees the whitewash on the back of his coat. He looks down at his gloves and puts them behind his back

Roger No more problems then, old mate?
Bob Only one, I can't play, not today, sorry.
Roger But you said you were all right.
Bob I said my back was all right. (*Shiftily*) No. It's Ginnie.
Roger *I* see.

They move outside

Bob Oh come on Rog, I know you've never liked her but ...
Roger Oh, why won't she let you play?
Bob It's not that who said it was that? No. She's not well. As a matter of fact, she's in bed. I just don't think I can leave her. Not all day.

A moment. Roger regards his gloves and sighs heavily

Roger Got a fag have you, Bob. I've given up.

Bob quickly pulls out a packet of cigarettes and offers one to Roger, who indicates the messy gloves. Bob puts a cigarette into Roger's mouth and lights it for him

Bob How long since you gave up?

Roger Nearly two weeks.

Bob Wish I could. Forty a day now.

Roger Willpower, I suppose. Mind you, Mim gave up at the same time which helped. (*He peels off the gloves and takes the cigarette from his mouth*)

Bob I feel rotten, you know that, Rog.

Roger Bad, is she?

Bob Pretty bad. Temperature and everything. I mean, you know women, they don't go to bed unless they're—you know.

Roger Because the thing is Bob, I've only got eleven. You don't play and I'm down to ten because I'm not borrowing, I'm not—I'm not borrowing one of their lot, not after the way they carried on last time; oh no. They could offer me Ian Bloody Botham and I wouldn't have him. I wouldn't Bob, I mean it.

Bob I know you wouldn't.

Roger I wouldn't.

Bob (*increasingly shifty*) I left it till this morning because I thought she might pull herself together but if anything she's even worse. That was who I was phoning just now, the doctor. Just sort of—you know. (*He sits on a bench*)

Roger What is it–flu?

Bob Er—more like a heavy cold.

Roger (*sitting next to Bob*) Here's what you do, then. You fetch her here, in the car, nice and warm, couple've blankets, nice drop of sunshine, clear her head do her the world of good, Mim'll look after her, give her a ring, see what she says ... (*He tries to drag Bob inside to the phone*)

Bob Well, I would do, Rog, but you know Ginnie, she might take it the wrong way, she's a bit funny like that. I really feel I should go back and look after her and—that's that really.

Bob moves to the steps. A moment, then Roger puts his arm around Bob's shoulders chummily and guides him so that they are both looking out over the pitch

Roger Flipping heck I quite understand, Bob—of course I do. If she's not well she's not well, not your fault, these things happen. Mim was ill once, I seem to remember. But I'd just like to say one thing. One last thing. Which is, I've come to depend on you. Out there I mean. That's all. We'll miss you. That's all. Especially with this lot coming set on thrashing us all round the park after what we did to 'em last year. It'll be a battle, that's all mate, and I would've liked you out there alongside me. Still. We'll be all right, my old mate.

Bob Christ, Rog, I feel terrible.

Roger No no no—we'll make out. Always have always will.

There is the sudden sound of someone whistling

Dennis!

Dennis enters from the car park. Dennis is in his mid-forties: tall, hair cut to disguise a thinning patch, face a little too florid from too many large whiskies at too many lunchtime sessions with prospective customers. Secondary modern school self-made sales manager with an "improved" accent. Too improved. His clothing is a little too sharp, includes a light blue denim cap. He carries a sports bag. When he first appears, he looks decidedly seedy: but seeing the other two, he braces himself and steps up breezily

Dennis Afternoon skip, afternoon old boy. (*Holding up his bag*) Any chance of a knock, is there?

Roger, his arm still around Bob, regards Dennis with a mixture of surprise and delight

Roger I thought you couldn't play this week?
Dennis Truth is, I suddenly thought to m'self, good God, what do I want with trailing round looking at houses? So I said to her, look love, you want to look at houses, you're quite capable of looking at the bloody things by yourself. So—(*with his big smile*)—if I'm too late for a knock, fair enough, bit of umpiring, whatever you fancy.

Roger rejects Bob and moves across to take Dennis's bag

Roger How d'you fancy a knock at number three?
Dennis (*withdrawing his bag*) Ah. Well ...
Roger Five?
Dennis (*letting Roger take the bag now*) Anywhere you fancy, old boy, you're the guv'nor.
Roger Five it is then. Super. Smashing. Good old Dennis.

Roger moves cheerfully inside, putting the bag on the floor and going to the board to strike out Bob's name and insert Dennis's. Dennis nips inside after him, popping a sweet into his mouth, a habit of his, and winking at Bob. We sense an immediate current of dislike between these two men: nothing in particular, purely instinctive

Dennis What's this then?
Roger (*writing*) Bob can't play.
Dennis Oh that's a bit of bad; not like you to let the side down, Bob, old boy.
Bob It so happens that my wife is rather ill. Well, a bit poorly.
Dennis A likely story.
Bob (*quickly, guiltily*) Waddaya mean, a likely story?
Dennis *I* think the beautiful Virginia is giving you a bit of stick—(*with a gross wink*)—send her round to your uncle Dennis, old boy, I'll soon have her straightened out. You've got to train 'em, you know. Not only do they expect it, they like it.
Bob Do they, do they really.
Dennis Ask Rog, he's got it all nicely organized haven't you Rog?
Roger (*staring at the list*) What? Oh. Yes.
Bob Ginnie is ill and five minutes ago *you* weren't playing either. (*He stubs out his cigarette violently into an ashtray*)
Dennis Don't get so aeriated, old boy—just pulling your leg, that's all, just pulling your leg. So then—what's on the agenda?

Bob The roller.
Dennis Ah. (*He stares out at the pitch*) Roller. Just the three of us, is it?
Bob No, just the two of you, I'm off.
Dennis Right then. Just have a quick jimmy riddle. (*He starts to exit into the changing-rooms then turns*) Oh yes—Rog—I've had a word with my contact and we can have all the equipment we need at ten percent below cost— pads, gloves, bats, the lot. (*He touches his nose*) Fixed it.

With another wink at Bob, Dennis exits to the changing-rooms

Roger Good old Dennis. Saves us a fortune, you know.
Bob Yes he has mentioned it.
Roger Yes, well, thanks for letting me know, Bob, you'll be off now, will you? (*He shoos Bob towards the door*)
Bob The thing is, Rog, I mean, it's not *definite*. I mean, another hour and she could be fine—(*he starts to move towards the board*)—and I'd quite fancy a knock at number ...
Roger (*guiding him towards the door*) Look, old mate, you pop off and look after her—you'll be much happier knowing we're not depending on you— okay? Super.

Dennis breezes in, zipping up his fly

Dennis Right!
Bob (*moving outside*) Yes—well—good game then, Dennis.

Dennis gives him a confident thumbs-up

Might see you later then, Rog, quick pint or something.
Dennis If you happen to bump into a brand-new BMW round the corner in the car park, please don't—it's mine. (*He gives Bob a big wink*)
Roger (*snapping into action*) Smashing, cheers Bob. (*To Dennis*) Where was I?
Dennis Roller.
Roger Ah yes. The roller.

Roger and Dennis stare out towards the dreaded roller. Bob moves dejectedly away

Bob Pity about the weather though.
Roger What?
Bob Forecast reckons rain. Still. What do they know?

Slightly cheerier, Bob exits to the car-park

Roger moves out on to the grass and stares fearfully up at the sky. Dennis, pleased at the thought that rain might stop play, whistles cheerfully for a moment

Dennis Any of the girls here yet?
Roger Sorry?
Dennis Mim here, is she? (*He lounges on a bench*)
Roger Er—she's—er—gone to get the thingies, the salad whatsits. You know, the wajamacallems, the sandwiches.

Roger dashes inside to take up the newspaper. Dennis mimes a creaky stroke of the bat

Dennis Just one thing, Rog, I know I haven't been doing too well with the old bat just lately but I really think I'm through all that, I really think I've found the answer, you know what I mean?

Roger (*reading*) "Further outlook continuing dry". What's he talking about? Flip. Flip, flip, *flip*. (*He drags his list out of his pocket, stabs a finger at it*) "Off-licence, Bob". I knew it, he was supposed to collect the beer. I dunno, some of these blokes, their women go down with something and they fall to pieces. (*Decisively again*) Right! You get the beer, I'll sort this lot out, okay?

Dennis Just the beer, is it?

Roger Quick as you like, there's still that roller. (*He moves towards the steps, but stops*) Super!

Roger hurries inside and into the bar, closing the door, still studying his list

Dennis stands dejectedly for a moment, then pulls himself together and starts to move to the car-park

Kevin enters moodily, followed by Maggie. Kevin is thirty. He is short, with long hair and a drinker's stomach which is constantly forcing a rift between trousers and shirt. Dress him how you like and he would never look tidy. His mood swings between world-weary resignation and fantastic enthusiasm. He carries a scruffy cricket bag with an airways sticker on it. Maggie is twenty-eight, and half a foot taller. She wears great big glasses for her genuine short sight, a red gash of lipstick, hair piled high on her head, an elderly box-shouldered fur-coat and high wedge shoes. Most of the time her hands remain firmly thrust into the deep coat pockets. She has a flat North London accent. A big untidy woman who is somehow extremely sexy—it is the way she care-lessly arranges her limbs. She has been married to Kevin for only a year and underneath all the surface banter, they adore each other

They meet up with Dennis, Maggie looking around, screwing up her nose as she focusses, clearly not having been here before

Dennis Afternoon old man. (*To Maggie, appraisingly*) Good afternoon.

Maggie Oh ... (*She focuses on him*) Hello.

Kevin Hello, Den. This is Maggie. (*He jerks a head*) Dennis.

Maggie Hello.

Dennis Well well well, pleased to meet you at last. Come to watch, have we?

Dennis is even creepier with women—always trying to impress and always failing

Kevin Silly cow, look what she gets herself up in. (*He slumps on a bench and pulls up his socks*)

Maggie (*to Dennis*) I hate draughts, don't you?

Kevin Draughts? What's she on about, draughts?

Maggie If you're sitting in a field, you're bound to get draughts.

Kevin Ask her what she's on about, will you?

Maggie He's not talking to me.

Dennis Oh I see—bit of a tiff.

Kevin Bit of a tiff? I'll bloody brain her. You know what she said? Go on—
tell him what you said, I dare you.

Maggie I said—I thought it would go further.

Kevin She thought it would go further. (*He shakes his head and mumbles his
way inside*) I even had to carry me own bag. What sort of woman is that,
I ask you? I give up, I do, I give up.

Kevin exits into the changing-rooms

*Maggie shrugs her great square shoulders at Dennis, who cannot quite make
her out—like a lot of people who make the mistake of thinking that her slow
rather emotionless voice and myopic gaze means that she is a bit dumb*

Dennis Look—if there's anything I can do.

He takes her hand paternally. She looks down to the hand then back up at him

Maggie How d'you mean?

Dennis Well—you know—I hate to see a young couple ...

Maggie Oh no, he'll be all right. He's just irritable 'cos he's missing his beer,
that's all.

Dennis Well there we are then you see ... (*He pats her hand*) I'm just going
to pick it up.

Maggie What?

Dennis The beer.

Maggie No, he's off it: that's why he's missing it. Tell you what though, you
can bring us back a bottle of wine.

Dennis *Mais certainement: le vin rouge?*

Maggie Yeah, white wine, German if you can. Here, I'll give you some money.

Dennis (*holding her hand and patting it again*) Give it to me later.

Maggie All right then, thankseversomuch.

*Dennis moves away towards the car-park, digging out his new car keys, and
whistling "I'm in the mood for love", suddenly inspired by this statuesque
young woman who has husband trouble. He exits*

*Maggie watches, nose wrinkled, as Dennis moves away. She moves slowly into
the pavilion, looking around, pushing her glasses up her nose, dabbing her nose
with a tissue and pulling the coat even tighter around herself. She sees the piano,
moves to it, raises the lid, bends down low over it and thumps out a tune, one
finger at a time*

*Kevin comes out of the changing rooms minus his bag and, pointedly ignoring
her, moves to examine the team list*

Maggie stops playing

I think it's colder in here.

Kevin Don't—waste—your—breath.

Maggie I'm not wasting it, I'm watching it turn into steam—look ... (*She
puffs out air through great rounded red lips*)

Kevin (*keeping his back to her*) I'm not talking to you.

She takes the darts from the dartboard and throws them expertly

Maggie Suit yourself.

Kevin In fact I'm not talking to you ever again.

Maggie My mum'll be pleased, she said you were a little twerp and I agree with her.

Kevin But before I never talk to you again, I'll just say this ... (*He moves to her menacingly so that they are chest to face*) You don't mess about with my cooking ... *I* don't mess about with your cement.

She sticks her tongue out at him, then suddenly has her arms around him, still with her hands in the coat pockets

Get off, you silly great cow.

Maggie Let me give you a cuddle, cheer you up.

He exaggeratedly fends her off as she is towering over him, the coat spread wide. He takes up one of the bar stools to defend himself

Kevin Get off, will you! I'm supposed to be the demon bowler—how can I dish out me off-spinners when I've been crushed to death in that lot ...

Maggie Come here, you little teddy-bear, you ...

She grabs the legs of the stool and forces it down so that she and Kevin are face to face and he seizes her coat threateningly

Kevin How many more times, I cannot stand violence!

She kisses him

The bar shutter is raised, and Roger appears behind the drinks bar

Roger Afternoon all. (*He seems unaware of their struggle*)

Kevin Oh hello, Rog. (*To Maggie*) This is Roger, he's the captain so a bit of respect.

Maggie Oh. Hello.

Kevin This is Maggie. I told you she was big, didn't I?

Maggie I'm not that big, am I?

Roger Err ...

Maggie Anyway, he likes me big. Don't you, you know you do.

She advances on Kevin, and he backs away

Kevin Get off, you great ... Get her off, Rog, she'll ruin me spinning finger.

Roger What I need—is a hand with the roller.

Kevin (*staring out towards the pitch*) The roller. I thought Alex was down to do the roller?

Roger He was but he he hasn't turned up.

Kevin Typical.

Maggie What's the roller?

Kevin (*sitting on a stool at the counter*) It's a great big heavy round thing that flattens everything in its path—a bit like you as a matter of fact. Here, Rog, she's bigger than I am, why can't she do it?

Roger Err ...

Maggie I don't mind. (*She moves myopically towards the steps, pushing back her sleeves*)
Roger Oh. Would you really?
Maggie Will if you like.
Kevin She would an'all, the great soft tart. (*He points a warning finger at her*) Don't you dare, you'll hurt yourself.
Maggie Ooo I love him, don't you just love him? Come here, I wanna give you a kiss. (*She sweeps Kevin off the stool as though he were an infant, arms and legs around her*)
Kevin Don't keep picking me up, woman!
Maggie Well, let me have a baby, then.
Kevin I don't want a baby.
Maggie Suit yourself. (*She drops him back onto the stool with a bang*)
Kevin (*sighing*) Maggie ...
Maggie Go on, go and roll your rotten pitch!

Kevin shrugs and, rubbing his behind, moves out and exits towards the pitch

(*Shouting after him*) And don't go on about buying me a cocker spaniel. I don't want a cocker rotten spaniel!

She stands, hands in pockets, glowering moodily as Roger comes out from behind the bar, holding his list

Roger Tell you what—if you want to do something, you could, er—you could—(*aware of her glowering*)—um—yes, well, Mim'll be back soon. (*He hurries after Kevin*) Wait for me, Kev!

Roger exits to the pitch

Maggie lounges on a bar stool, digging out a tissue to wipe her nose. She is doing so when the phone rings. She wrinkles her nose towards it, focusing. Unhurriedly she looks around, then moves unhurriedly across to the phone, rather like a giraffe in slow motion, and takes up the receiver

Maggie (*on the phone*) Hello? ... No it isn't it's Maggie who's that? ... Who? ... Don't think so, I'm the only one here at the minute ... Yes, all right, I'll tell him ... Bye.

During the above, Miriam enters carrying a box full of lettuces, cucumbers, etc. She moves into the pavilion, makes to go into the kitchen, but becomes aware of Maggie and turns

Miriam (*brightly*) Hello. I'm Miriam, Roger's wife, who are you?
Maggie Oh hello, I'm Maggie.
Miriam Maggie?
Maggie Kevin's wife. (*She holds out a hand at chest height*)
Miriam Oh—*Maggie*—I'm so sorry. How nice to meet you at last.

Miriam extends a hand and they shake hands

Maggie I've heard all about you.
Miriam That's nice. I hope.
Maggie All about you and your fantastic spreads.

Miriam (*somewhat disappointed*) Well—you've chosen a super day. We thought he was hiding you away or something.
Maggie Now why would he want to do that?
Miriam Just a—figure of speech actually, I didn't ...

Maggie replaces the bar stool Kevin was fending her off with

Maggie Saturdays I usually get on with the house.
Miriam Yes, Kevin said. You haven't been there long, have you?
Maggie Not long, no. That's why I don't mind him playing his silly cricket. Gives me a chance to get on.
Miriam They are inclined to get under your feet, aren't they?
Maggie Specially when they're as little as he is. Little but perfect. Oooo, I love him.

Miriam smiles weakly: embarrassed as she always is when dealing with anything that might spank of the physical

Miriam (*moving behind the counter*) Would you mind if I got on?
Maggie I'll give you a hand if you like.
Miriam Would you mind? I mean, it's not compulsory.
Maggie Whatever you fancy, keep me out of mischief, won't it?
Miriam Super. (*She starts to guide Maggie behind the counter*)
Maggie Oh yeah, some woman phoned. She thought I was you—Jilly is it?
Miriam Jilly? Ginnie would it be—Bob's wife?
Maggie That's it, Bob's wife. She said to tell him he's left his bag behind.
Miriam Isn't he here?
Maggie Dunno—is he?
Miriam He was—I expect Roger's organized him into doing something energetic. Would you like to take your coat off first?
Maggie No not really. I suffer terrible from the draught.
Miriam Oh. That's nasty for you.
Maggie Once it goes to me chest I've had it. I'd wear a vest, but he'd only tear it.

Miriam smiles weakly

Maggie and Miriam exit to the kitchen. Dennis staggers round the corner under the weight of two crates of beer. He moves into the pavilion, looking out towards the pitch with a brave smile indicating "look, I've got the beer" and staggers inside, as Miriam comes out of the kitchen, moving to take up the box of salad from the counter

Miriam Well now, Maggie, if you'd like to be doing this salad ... (*She sees Dennis and moves to helpfully open the bar door for him*)
Dennis (*breathlessly*) Hello Mim, old love.
Miriam Let me give you a hand

She holds the door open and stands to one side as he staggers behind the bar, puts down the crates and comes out again, mopping palms with his handkerchief and smiling bravely

Dennis Two down, four to go.
Miriam I didn't think you were playing this week, Dennis.
Dennis (*winking*) Couldn't do without me, could they?

He puts an arm around her, squeezes her, and makes to plant a kiss on her brow—which embarrasses her beyond belief, so that she pulls away from him but tries to make it light

Miriam Steady the buffs, I'm a married woman.

She moves towards the counter and he moves after her, hands outstretched, and speaking in a cod-french accent

Dennis Of course you are, and you're crazy about me, you know you are.

He catches up with her and puts his arms around her, tickling her. She giggles, trying to pull away

> *Maggie enters from the kitchen*

Caught in the act!
Miriam (*disengaging herself with a bright smile*) This is Dennis. He's in carpets.
Maggie We've already met. Can you get things wholesale?
Dennis That depends, doesn't it, Mim?

He squeezes Miriam with his leery smile and she holds her bright smile, but disengages herself

Maggie Is this the salad you want washing?
Miriam I'm so sorry, I was helping Dennis with the beer.
Maggie Oh. I'll get out of your way then, shall I?

> *Maggie takes up the box and goes back into the kitchen*

Dennis (*referring to Maggie*) Be warm enough d'you think?
Miriam I wish you hadn't done that, Dennis. I know it's just a bit of fun and everything but—I just can't cope with things like that. I don't know why, I sort of ... (*Annoyed with herself*) Oh God, listen to me.

He looks at her, then—as Good Old Dependable Uncle Dennis—pulls out cigarettes and offers her one. Sorely tempted, she almost takes it, then waves it away

Dennis Bit tense are we, old love?
Miriam I'm fine, fine. (*Her bright smile returns and she snaps back into action*) Oh well, best be getting on, I suppose.
Dennis (*in an impersonation of Roger*) No time for idle chatter, things to be done, chop chop.

Miriam offers the best smile she can manage and goes behind the counter, as Dennis moves outside, lighting a cigarette

Miriam (*calling*) Oh—if you see Bob, will you tell him Ginnie rang.
Dennis Bob? He's been and gone, old love.

Miriam Oh, that's all right then. He obviously hadn't got there when she phoned.

Dennis Something up?

Miriam He forgot his bag, that's all. (*She starts to go into the kitchen*)

Dennis You mean she phoned to say he'd left his bag behind?

Miriam Didn't he say?

Dennis Oh well. Nothing to do with me, is it? (*He gives her a big phoney smile and moves quickly out on to the grass*)

Miriam Dennis... (*She follows him outside, moving to him*) There's nothing—funny going on is there, Dennis? Because if there is, I think, as Roger's wife, I ought to know.

Dennis (*heaving a sigh, but relishing the situation*) Well, I can't see why she should phone to say he's left his bag behind when half-an-hour ago he was here saying he couldn't play because Ginnie was ill in bed and he had to look after her.

A moment. Then Miriam sits slowly on the bench

Miriam You know it really isn't fair, involving other people in his—goings-on.

Dennis (*sitting close to her*) Mustn't jump to conclusions now, must we, Mim?

Miriam He makes me so—angry.

Dennis He makes me laugh.

Miriam Honestly—so angry.

Dennis Would've thought he'd have learned his lesson by now. But here he is, at it again apparently. Wouldn't be so bad if he didn't keep falling in love and marrying 'em. Must be costing him a fortune.

Miriam What are we going to do?

Dennis Nothing we can do, old love.

Miriam Apart from anything else, it's letting Roger down. He's trying to run a team, not a ... I mean, you know how upset he was last time, he was very fond of Bob's first wife. I can see the whole thing happening again only this time it'll be Ginnie blaming him ... Oh damn. Damn, damn, damn.

Dennis (*taking her hand*) It'll be all right. Promise.

Miriam (*extricating the hand*) I'd rather you didn't say anything to Roger—you know how upset he gets when he feels—you know—let down.

Dennis (*giving the scout's signal*) Cross my heart.

Dennis exits to the car-park, grinning with some satisfaction at Bob's problem. Maggie comes out of the kitchen

Maggie All done.

Miriam (*hurrying inside*) Oh, I'm so sorry.

Maggie No skin off my nose—anything else, is there—or what?

Miriam Well—if you'd like to give me a hand with the table.

Maggie I'd rather have a game o' darts.

Miriam Oh—well—(*brightly*)—it's not compulsory you know.

Maggie Cor, Miriam, you ain't 'arf a one—which table, this one?

Maggie and Miriam set up the trestle table, and Maggie pulls a folding screwdriver from her pocket and tightens one of the screws on the leg during the following

Mind you, I'd be working on the house today only I ran out of sharp sand and the rotten devils wouldn't deliver.

Miriam Sharp?

Maggie Sand. I'm laying some new paths round the back.

Miriam Oh. *(All she can think of to say)* Are you any good at it?

Maggie Not bad. My father was a master brickie.

Miriam Was he?

Maggie You sort of pick these things up, don't you?

Miriam Yes, I suppose you do. What's a brickie?

Maggie Bricklayer. He was fantastic, my old dad, a joy to watch.

Miriam They're so terribly hard to get hold of nowadays, aren't they, decent craftsmen.

Maggie Oh there's a lot of cowboys about. Still—if ever there's anything you want done, give us a ring and if I'm not busy I'll see you're all right. *(She hoists herself on to one of the stools and starts to roll a cigarette)*

Miriam Oh—well—I mean—thank you. And if there's ever any typing you need done ...

Maggie Mind you, Kevin's the one for grub.

Miriam Is he?

Maggie Have you never tasted his cooking?

Miriam I had no idea.

Maggie Self-taught-very-nearly-*cordon-bleu*, my little Kev.

Miriam Gosh.

Maggie His kitchen is his kingdom and he rules it with a rod of iron. Well, tube of spaghetti actually.

Miriam Roger doesn't know where the kitchen is.

Maggie Me, I'm useless! Toast and marmalade and that's about my lot.

Miriam Perhaps I should compare notes with him.

Maggie Toast and marmalade and sex. They're the only things I'm any good at.

Miriam offers a weak smile and quickly moves to take up her duster and dust the keys of the piano which tinkle tinkle tinkle

Dennis staggers on carrying another two crates—cigarette sticking out of his mouth, back bent—and goes behind the drinks bar to deposit the crates

Dennis All right, ladies?

Miriam Dennis is really very sweet, you know. He gets most of the team equipment wholesale—Roger often says he doesn't know what he'd do without him.

Maggie Oh yeah? *(She sniffs, gropes for a tissue and runs the back of her hand across her nose)* 'Scuse me, I've left my tissues.

Maggie goes into the kitchen

Dennis comes wearily from behind the bar

Miriam Shirley be coming, will she Dennis?

Dennis Shirley, God bless her, is having a lovely time looking at houses. (*He starts to move outside*)

Miriam You are moving then? Oh, she will be pleased.

Dennis (*psuedo-confidentially*) Between you me and the building society—no Mim, we are not moving. That is to say, I am not moving. Now Shirley may think we're moving—Shirley may think anything she likes—but—no. (*He rams the fag back into his mouth and moves away*)

Miriam Then why is she looking at houses?

Dennis (*stopping and turning*) Because she likes looking at houses. It makes her happy. And I do like her to be happy, dear old soul.

Dennis exits to the car-park, as Maggie comes out of the kitchen dabbing her nose with a tissue

Miriam (*moving back inside*) He was just saying—his wife won't be coming.

Maggie Oh yeah?

Miriam She's house-hunting.

Maggie And the best of British.

Miriam They haven't been moved long actually. (*She goes into the kitchen and calls*) One of these "executive estates", I think they call them.

Maggie I know: those places where young people go to die.

Miriam returns with a plastic pot of cutlery which she individually wipes with a cloth. Maggie sits on one of the stools and stretches one of her legs out to rest on the other stool as she lights her rolled cigarette

I'm all for Victorian an' that m'self. More work admittedly, but at least you feel you're in a house.

Miriam Lovely high ceilings and everything, yes I agree. We're rather lucky actually ...

Maggie, having lit her cigarette, flicks the match on to the floor. Miriam leans over the counter pointedly

Oops ...

Maggie follows her eyeline and bends myopically to search for the match, which she finds, and Miriam takes from her and deposits tidily in a bin as she continues speaking

Yes, nineteen-twenties ours is—early nineteen-twenties—a semi unfortunately, but lovely and solid and a really super garden.

Maggie Do they usually come then—the women?

Miriam (*polishing the cutlery busily*) Depends really. Some do, some don't. Depends really. I have to. No, that sounds awful. I mean I don't have to— enjoy it. Really. It's a sort of break—especially as most Saturdays we pack the children off to grandma which means that Rog and I can have the whole day together. We've always done things together, ever since college. We're very lucky, touch wood, we enjoy being together. Sharing things. Sort of— equal partners as it were. It's rather super really.

Roger (*off, shouting*) Miriam!

Miriam (*jumping up and hurrying from behind the counter*) Yes, darling!

Roger enters irritably from the pitch

Roger Blisters!
Miriam What about blisters, darling?
Roger Don't mess me about, Mim, what do you *do* with them?

Kevin follows Roger in, holding up an "injured" hand before him

Maggie What's happened?
Kevin I've only blistered me entire *raison d'être*.
Maggie Your what?
Kevin Me spinning finger, you great lump.
Maggie (*in pseudo-horror*) Oo-er, not his *spinning* finger!
Roger I'm afraid so.
Maggie Come here, let me kiss it better.
Kevin (*defending himself exaggeratedly*) Don't touch me!
Roger Miriam!
Miriam Yes, darling?
Roger Remind me to make a note: "Must get some grease on that roller."

During the above, Dennis staggers round with two more crates which he lugs up the steps

Dennis (*though no-one has even looked at him*) It's all right, I can manage.

Dennis goes behind the bar

Maggie (*sitting on the steps*) I knew you should've let me do the rotten roller— let me see it.
Kevin (*sitting next to her*) There.
Maggie Where?
Kevin (*pointing*) *There.*
Maggie (*peering close, raising her glasses*) It's a blister.
Kevin I know it's a blister, you silly great haystack.
Roger The best thing is not to panic.
Miriam The best thing, if I might suggest, is to cover it up.
Roger (*pointing*) Cover it up.
Maggie Cover it up.
Kevin What with?
Roger Yes, what with?
Miriam Elastoplast.
Maggie He's allergic to Elastoplast.
Kevin *Penicillin*, you great . . .
Miriam Yes, I'd definitely cover it up.
Maggie I'll do it, shall I?
Kevin If you value cleverly-flighted off-breaks, you'll keep her away from me.
Roger Come on now, Mim, you're the First Aid Department, chop chop.
Miriam Please don't tell me to chop chop, Roger.
Kevin It's beginning to throb.
Maggie It could be a blackman's pinch.

Kevin (*pointing to his finger*) Look! You can see it.
Miriam Cold water.
Roger Where is it?
Miriam In the tap, darling.
Roger The *Elastoplast*.
Miriam In the car.

Dennis staggers wearily from the bar, mopping his brow

Roger Right! You busy at the moment, Dennis?
Dennis Err—no, not particularly, skip.
Roger (*to Miriam*) Keys.

Miriam hurries to collect the keys from the counter

Dennis (*to Maggie*) I got the you-know.
Maggie Pardon?
Dennis (*"nudge nudge wink wink"*) The old vino del plonk.

Miriam passes the keys to Roger who almost snatches them and gives them to Dennis

Roger In the car, thanksverymuch.
Dennis Right. (*He starts to go*)
Miriam Dennis ...
Dennis Yes, old love?
Miriam Glove compartment, under the Guide Michelin.
Dennis Right. (*He starts off again, then stops*) What is?
Roger *Elastoplast!*
Dennis Someone in the wars, are they?
Maggie It's my little Kevin's finger.
Dennis (*joking*) Not his spinning finger I trust?
Roger (*deadly serious*) The very same.
Kevin (*holding up his finger*) Look at that.
Dennis Oh, right, fair enough.

Dennis exits as quickly as his exhausted frame will allow

Kevin Shall I put it under the tap or what?

Miriam starts to guide him into the changing-rooms

Miriam Come along, there's a brave little soldier.
Kevin Eh?
Miriam Oh—sorry.
Maggie Come on, sunshine—through here, is it? (*She guides him into the changing-rooms*)
Kevin Leggo my arm, you're cutting off the circulation, you great ...

Maggie puts a hand on the back of Kevin's head and shoves him through the door as though he were a small boy, and they go

Miriam Please don't say chop chop to me, Roger, it's bad enough in front of the children.

Roger (*staring, preoccupied, out at the pitch*) I'll tell you this, Miriam: the consequences of that blister could be appalling. Bob's the only other decent spinner we've got.

Miriam (*making it light*) You never did tell me what he meant, did you darling?

Roger (*still preoccupied*) What?

Miriam Pushover. Bit of a pushover.

Roger Miriam—in approximately one hour from now I shall be leading my team against the combined and slightly more than belligerent might of The British Railways Maintenance Division Yeading East. Now I know for a fact that five of that lot are genuine West Indians and shit-hot. I don't ask you for much, Miriam, but what I am asking for now is peace of mind.

Dennis enters, breathless, with the Elastoplast

Miriam Thank you so much, Dennis.

Dennis My pleasure old love. (*He slumps on a bench*) Phew, it's going to be a right old stinker. (*He mops his brow, his cap awry*)

Roger (*snapping a finger at him*) Just get the bag out of the boot and we're bang up to schedule ... (*Suddenly goes back to shout*) Love you, okay?

Roger guides the weary Dennis round to the car-park and they exit

Miriam sorts out strips of Elastoplast

Kevin enters from the changing-rooms

Kevin (*shouting back*) I'm not talking to you! (*To Miriam*) Will you please tell that woman to stop picking me up and putting me down where I don't want to be put down.

Miriam (*with her uncertain smile*) Where is she?

Kevin I dunno—mucking about in the ladies'.

Miriam glances uneasily in that direction and Kevin wipes the back of a hand across his mouth

I couldn't half do with a nice pint.

Miriam Oh—well—um—there *is* some beer if you ...

Kevin (*holding up a hand*) I've given it up. (*He thumps his large semi-naked stomach*) Watcha think of that? Solid as a rock that is. I've cut out the beer and joined the *Sunday Times* Wine Club—go on—feel it ...

Miriam Well yes, I can see it's very—um ...

Kevin Go on, *feel* it—solid as a rock ...

He takes her hand and presses it against his stomach underneath his shirt-front

Maggie enters

Miriam is once again vaguely aware of being caught

Miriam Kevin was just showing me his stomach.

Maggie I hope you don't mind, I just adjusted your ballcock.

Miriam Oh—thanks awfully, I'll tell Rog.

Kevin Excuse me—(*holding up the finger*)—what about this?

Miriam Sit down, please.
Kevin Why?
Miriam Because I'm going to do your plaster.
Kevin I won't faint, y'know.
Miriam It's better for Mim if you sit down.

Kevin jumps up to sit on the trestle table. Miriam fixes a plaster for him and he is awfully brave. Maggie drifts over to the dartboard to take the darts from it. She throws them rather expertly at the board

Kevin Why did I ever get married? I was much happier on my own. She tricked me, y'know. Told me she was a man of property. And you know what she's done now, don't you? Go on, ask her, I dare you.
Maggie I got Shanghaid once—just like that. (*She mimes throwing*) Boom boom boom ...
Kevin I made some beautiful chicken soup last night, and you know what she's done, the dozy great lump, she's only put milk in it. Milk. I could kill her.
Maggie Well I didn't know, did I?
Miriam Not *milk* though, Maggie.
Kevin You know what she said—go on—ask her what she said, I dare you.
Miriam What did you say?
Maggie I said I thought it would go further.
Kevin She thought it would go further. My chicken soup. I give up, I do, I give up.
Miriam (*finishing the plaster*) How's that?
Kevin (*regarding the plaster mournfully*) I think that's me finished, that's what I think.
Maggie What d'you mean, that's you finished?

Roger and Dennis appear, lugging the large and tatty team bag between them

Roger One, two, three—go.

Roger immediately lets go of the bag and Dennis' arm is almost pulled from its socket. Dennis slumps on to the bench, and Roger bustles inside

Right then—Kevin, give Dennis a hand into the changing room, there's a good chap.

Miriam goes behind the drinks bar

Maggie Careful of his *raison d'être.*

Dennis heaves himself wearily to his feet, and he and Kevin lug the bag through into the changing-rooms—Dennis finding enough strength to wink at Maggie en route

Roger Miriam!
Miriam Scoreboard—yes, darling—I was just about to do it.
Roger That's all right then, That's all right. (*With a hint of petulance*) Where *is* everyone, in the pub I suppose.

Roger exits to the changing-rooms

Maggie Stone me, what a palaver. I thought it was just a matter of putting on a pair of white strides and kicking a silly little ball about.

Miriam Mustn't let Rog hear you say that—gosh no, there's lots more.

Maggie (*flatly*) Triffic.

Miriam Oh yes—tons.

Maggie D'you want me to do anything?

Miriam There *is* a tablecloth in a plastic bag in the kitchen—you could start laying that if you like.

Maggie I expect I could finish laying it an' all if I really tried.

Miriam (*with a sort of gay little laugh*) Oh ... yes ... super.

Maggie exits into the kitchen

Miriam takes up a folded canvas chair from just inside the drinks bar and hurries outside to set up the chair in front of the scoreboard, goes back inside and sees Dennis' bag where Roger left it

(*Tut-tutting lightly*) Dennis ...

Miriam carries the bag through into the changing-rooms as Maggie comes out of the kitchen with the tablecloth which she unhurriedly spreads over the table. Ginnie appears round the corner. Ginnie is in her mid-thirties. An attractive woman whose way of coping with most situations she does not enjoy is to assume a mantle of languid superiority. Actually, she is on Valium. She speaks with a faint Northern accent and wears sunglasses, a simple but expensive summer dress, expensive sandals revealing painted toenails. She carries a cricket bag, a folded sun-lounger and a large beachbag. She surveys the dreaded scene

Ginnie Oh God. (*She shudders slightly and sets down the sun lounger, looking up at the sky*)

Miriam comes out of the changing-rooms with the scorebook and busies outside—not seeing Ginnie

Which is the east would you say?

Miriam (*staring*) Ginnie.

Ginnie Yes, darling, it's me, the scourge of Sainsbury's. Where did you say the east was?

Miriam Would you excuse me for a moment?

Before Ginnie can protest, Miriam hurries inside: Ginnie's arrival has thrown her completely. She peers round the corner as Ginnie sets up the sun-lounger with some difficulty

Maggie What's up?

Miriam Ginnie's here. But she never comes ...

Maggie Who?

Miriam (*in a hiss*) Bob's wife. Ginnie.

Maggie Oh, the one who phoned up.

Miriam What am I going to say to her?

Maggie Difficult to get on with, is she?

Miriam But it's so unfair, involving other people. (*She moves close to Maggie*) You haven't seen him, all right?

Maggie Seen who?

Miriam (*pointing towards the verandah*) Bob.

Maggie But I haven't seen him, have I? Where is he, this Bob?

Miriam That's what he's like you see. It's so unfair. (*She is almost wringing her hands with concern*) You see, she and Roger have never really hit it off because *she* thinks—Ginnie—that Roger blames her for breaking up Bob's family—Bob was married before you see and it's really Bob that Rog was sort of angry with because when he was married and going off with Ginnie he said he was playing cricket which he wasn't and, oh God, I can see it happening all again, all those horrible *atmospheres*—so please, don't say anything, not to Roger, not to anyone, not until I've sorted something out, promise?

Maggie listens to all this with her mouth open

Maggie Oh I do, I do.

Miriam hurries to the door, pauses to settle herself, and goes out on to the verandah with her over-bright smile as Maggie shrugs and gets on with laying the cloths

Miriam I've just had a word with Maggie and she says the sun sinks slowly in the west which makes the east sort of vaguely over there. (*She points vaguely*)

Maggie sits on a stool and rolls a cigarette

Ginnie Who's Maggie?

Miriam Kevin's wife.

Ginnie She's awfully well-made, isn't she?

Miriam She's terribly nice, actually. Terribly helpful. And a really good brickie, I believe.

Ginnie Really.

Miriam Her father was one and she sort of picked it up—well you do, don't you? (*Suddenly*) Why are you here?

Ginnie Hopefully to lie in the sun.

Miriam But you haven't been all season, why have you come today?

Ginnie Thank you, dearie.

Miriam No, I didn't mean it like that ...

Ginnie No, you're absolutely right. And I wouldn't be here today had it not been for that nasty little man next door and his sodding great bonfire. I'm sure there's a law or something about lighting fires on a Saturday—especially a Saturday like this—(*head back to the sun*)—God, isn't it wonderful? How often do we get a day like this?

Miriam Not often, I'm glad to say.

Ginnie Of course, you're not a sun-person, are you? (*She slaps her upper arm and dips into the beachbag to pull out a huge anti-insect aerosol spray, which she wafts generously around herself*) Anyway, I thought I'd bring his silly bag and enjoy a spot of sun here—where is he, the fool?

Miriam Oh ... (*She makes a vague gesture in the general direction of every-where*)
Ginnie I assume he's popped off somewhere.
Miriam Bob? (*She smiles gaily at the thought*)
Ginnie Oh come off it, darling, he's always popping off somewhere, you know he is. It's all that nervous energy that's so attractive until you have to live with it.
Miriam Actually, he's—umm ... (*Again she makes the vague gesture*)
Ginnie Well, his car isn't here.
Miriam No, it wouldn't be, because he's taken it with him. I remember now, he's getting something for Roger. Some grease for the roller actually. After what happened to Kevin's finger.

Ginnie flits a hand over the lounger and sits, making herself comfortable, head back

Ginnie I suppose now I'm here I should give you a hand.
Miriam (*gaily*) It's not compulsory, you know.
Ginnie Right then. I'll keep out of your way. (*She delves into the bag and pulls out a massive paperback, well-thumbed—opens it about halfway through—but smiles up at Miriam*) Don't hesitate to give me a shout if you want me to butter a piece of bread or anything.

Miriam hovers a moment, then goes inside

Maggie Anything else?
Miriam Sorry?
Maggie (*referring to the table*) I've finished.

Miriam is about to reply

Roger and Kevin come out of the changing-rooms. Both looking depressed, Kevin holding a cricket ball.

Miriam (*anxious to avoid Roger*) Oh—yes—super—if you'd like to ...

Miriam moves quickly into the kitchen. Maggie shrugs and slopes after her, dabbing her nose with a tissue

Roger (*after Miriam and Maggie have gone*) You really think that's it, then, Kev?
Kevin It's an artificial aid, isn't it? They'll take one look at this plaster and scream blue murder about it being an artificial aid to increase my spinning potential. (*Sighing*) You could say Rog—that this plaster on my finger has become the metabolic steroid on my Achilles heel. Couldn't you?
Roger (*sighing*) Yes I suppose you could really. Got a fag have you Kev, I've given up.

Kevin pulls out a packet of cigarettes and gives one to Roger

Kevin How long?
Roger Nearly three weeks. Mim gave up at the same time. I decided we'd give it up together.
Kevin They'll scream blue murder, they will, I know they will.

Roger puts an arm around Kevin's shoulders and does his all-pals-together bit

Roger The thing is, of course Kev, that you're the only decent spinner we've got. I mean, there's only ever been you and Bob and he's not playing.

Kevin I'm not saying I won't play, Rog, what I'm saying is, I can't bowl. What I'm saying, Rog—(*nobly*)—is—maybe I should stand down and give someone else a chance to turn his arm over. For the sake of the team—that's what I think I should do.

Kevin puts the ball into Roger's hand, noble and insincere. Roger puts his arm even tighter around Kevin's shoulders and guides him towards the outside

Roger Listen to me, old mate. I've come to depend on you. Out there, I mean. And if there's one bloke I know I could depend on to lay down his life with the bat—recognized batsman or no recognized batsman—you know who that bloke would be, don't you mate? That's all I want to say, all right mate? Okay? (*He returns the ball to Kevin and guides him outside, arm still around his shoulder, towards the pitch*) What I'm saying is—it's up to you, mate ...

Ginnie lowers her sunglasses and peers at them

Ginnie D'you mind? You're frightening away my sun.

Roger, preoccupied, flutters fingers at her and continues directly

Roger What I'm saying is—it's your finger—but it's our team—what I'm saying is ... (*He suddenly realizes*) Virginia!

Ginnie Yes, Roger, it's me, The Prodigal Supporter. Hello Kevin, you really must give Bob the name of your tailor.

Roger rejects Kevin and moves across to sit next to Ginnie. Kevin slumps into the canvas chair moodily

Roger How *are* you, Virginia: in yourself I mean?

Ginnie, assuming his dislike of her, cannot help but be a little suspicious

Ginnie I'm fine: how are you in yourself?

Kevin *I've* got a bad finger. (*He holds it up*)

Roger Is Bob with you?

Ginnie Somewhere—something about some grease. (*She vaguely indicates the direction vaguely indicated by Miriam earlier*)

Roger Good old Bob! You are staying, are you?

Ginnie I sincerely hope so, dearie—I'm certainly not lugging this lot around any more—bonfire or no bonfire.

Roger (*suddenly awfully serious*) What I mean is—you're all right are you Virginia? No nasty side effects.

Ginnie Just a pair of watery eyes and a slight cough—why are you so concerned?

Roger Because I'd hate to think good old Bob dragged you out of bed for my sake.

Ginnie No, no, I often get up in the morning. Why? Has Good Old Bob been complaining?

Miriam and Maggie enter from the kitchen. Maggie remains behind the counter and goes back into the kitchen during the following

Roger The thing is—you're here. You're here and Bob's here and that's all that matters. But you *must* look after yourself. (*He moves to door and shouts*) Miriam!

Miriam, fearing the worst, moves to him instantly

Miriam Yes darling?

Roger Virginia's here. Now, she won't admit this, but I know she has risen from her bed to be here today. Now *I* think that's really rather special.

Ginnie I really must have a word with Good Old Bob.

Roger Miriam!

Miriam Yes darling.

Roger Look after her. Anything she wants. Blankets, lemon tea, aspirin, hot water bottle—anything.

Ginnie Roger darling—all I need is less smoke and more sun.

Roger (*pacing*) You heard that, Miriam—*no cigarettes. (He realizes he is holding one and hides it behind his back and takes a deep breath*) Fresh air and sunshine. Mother Nature Knows Best I always say—all right Miriam, okay? Super. All right, Kev, okay, happy now? (*He starts to move inside*) Tell you what Kev—now you're here you might fancy a spot of umpiring, see how you feel. (*Without waiting for an answer he moves to the team list, crosses out Kevin's name and inserts Bob's*)

Ginnie I would like to make it quite clear that, contrary to rumour, I often get up in the morning. Not always, but often.

Miriam hovers, desperately trying to pluck up courage to tell Roger the situation. Ginnie pointedly returns to her paperback. Kevin sits looking moodily at his finger

Dennis comes out of the changing-rooms, now in his cricket gear, but still wearing his jacket. He is lighting another cigarette

Kevin (*to Ginnie*) I'm not bloody umpiring, that's for sure.

Miriam moves quickly to Dennis and guides him to look down at Ginnie

Miriam Look Dennis, Virginia's here, isn't that super?

Ginnie Apparently it's more of a miracle. Hello Dennis.

Miriam (*gripping Dennis' arm*) Bob's—playing—you see.

Dennis Bob?

Miriam Yes, Bob. He's playing, yes.

Dennis Bob? He's playing?

Miriam (*nodding frantically*) Yes.

Dennis (*catching on, with some pleasure*) And you've come along to watch him, Virginia.

Miriam Yes, isn't it super?

Ginnie Oh my God.

Dennis (*grinning, stuffing his cigarette in his mouth*) Super.

Alex and Sharon enter from the car-park. Alex is in his early twenties. Tall, rather weakly good-looking, hair prematurely receding. Too much money and not awfully aware of anything outside himself. He wears good cashmere and white shoes and carries a leather holdall. A public schoolboy who has played at Lords: just the sort of chap Dennis feels he should associate with. Sharon is the girl he met two nights ago at a disco. She is a stunning nineteen-year-old blonde, dressed in what she hopes is right for an afternoon's cricket—all white with a big white hat and hopelessly over-dressed. She is happiest at the disco where you do not have to talk much. Right now she is paralysed with nerves at having to meet Alex's smart friends because she knows she has done it all wrong. She holds before her Alex' laundered cricket whites which are under a plastic bag on a hanger

Alex (*as they enter*) Last time I was here I scored sixty-three ...
Dennis (*moving to Alex*) Alex! Nice to see you.

Dennis unnecessarily pumps Alex's hand as Sharon remains to one side, cringing, with a big fixed smile. Alex moves away to stare out at the pitch

Alex Track's looking a bit brown—whose is the BMW?
Dennis Nice?
Alex Very nice—yours?
Dennis Finally did it—(*with a nudge*)—if you recommend a motor, that's good enough for Uncle Dennis.

Roger moves towards the doors and Dennis turns his "charm" on Sharon

And who is this delightful little mademoiselle?
Alex This is Sharon ...

He beckons Sharon to him with crooked finger. She dutifully moves to him and he takes the hanger from her

She's come along to watch me make another fifty or so, haven't you, poppet?
Kevin Big-headed poofter.
Roger That's what I like to hear—confidence. (*He sits on a bench, rubbing his hands together with pleasure at the arrival of his star player*)
Alex (*moving up the steps*) Shocking bloody pile-up on the by-pass. Drop of sun and they all turn out like K Registration lemmings.
Ginnie (*pointedly*) Hello, Sharon, I'm Virginia.

Sharon sits to one side on a bench

Alex Where's that Bob? I've got a bone to pick with him—bugger damn nigh ran me out last week ... (*He turns as if to look for Bob*)

Miriam hurries out and into action

Miriam (*quickly*) Well now, Sharon—introductions. (*Brightly and very quickly*) This is Kevin, he's got a bad finger—
Kevin —and he's not bloody umpiring—
Miriam —his wife is called Maggie and she's terribly nice and she's inside setting out the thingies—it isn't compulsory but every little does help and

I expect you'll want to do a little something yourself, won't you? Dennis
is the one with the new BMW and his wife is called Shirley and she's terribly
nice and usually helps out but she can't today because she's looking for
a new house—

Dennis (*winking at Sharon*) Or so she thinks ...

Miriam —this is Virginia—well, she's just said so, hasn't she and she's married
to Bob who's sort of over there—(*vaguely indicating*)—doing things.

Roger (*to Ginnie*) Plenty of hot drinks, that's the ticket.

Miriam Now then, where was I? Oh yes, I'm here and my name is Miriam
and I'm married to Roger who's the sort of captain.

Roger stands

No, I mean he is the captain. The others aren't here yet but when they do
come you'll see how awfully nice they are. (*She beams around*) There now.

Ginnie sprays her aerosol

Alex I'll get changed then.

*Alex never says anything directly to Sharon. He moves towards the changing-
rooms, and Roger goes after him*

Roger Now here's the situation as I see it. Paddy can't play this week so if
it's all right with you I'm moving Jeremy up to take first knock which should
work out okay because ...

Roger and Alex exit into the changing-rooms

Miriam beckons to Dennis

Miriam Dennis, I wonder if you could spare me a moment?

Dennis (*leaning over Sharon*) Duty calls.

   *Maggie moves out of the kitchen as Miriam beckons Dennis to follow her
   through. Miriam and Dennis exit to the kitchen*

*Ginnie returns to her book. Sharon sits unhappily on the bench, staring down
at her handbag. Kevin sits on the bench looking moodily at his finger. Maggie
drifts out and stands on the steps. She sees Sharon*

Maggie Hello.

Sharon (*instantly*) I've come from East Molesley.

Maggie I don't blame you.

Sharon (*standing and moving just a little closer to them*) Saturdays I usually
go shopping with me mum because me dad's still on crutches on account
of the accident. Well I *call* him me dad, but you know. They were going
to Broadstairs this week-end but they had to cancel it.

Maggie Well they would, wouldn't they?

Ginnie I would have thought so, yes.

Sharon It's ever so nice here, isn't it, with all the trees and everything? He's
ever such a good dancer, isn't he, Alex, but I was quite surprised when he
said he played cricket, well, you don't think, do you? Excuse me, I want
to get something out of the car.

Sharon hurries quickly away round the corner, almost in tears at her social incompetence

Ginnie I've got an awful feeling she's gone to fetch her album. Oh God, I just know she's going to pass round photographs of assorted relatives.
Maggie She looked more to me like she's going to pass out.
Ginnie Hardly surprising, is it, dear—day like today and five hundred yards of muslin. I suppose he did tell her it's cricket and not Come Dancing?
Kevin They won't let me play, you know that, don't you?
Maggie What d'you mean—they won't let you play?

She moves over to where he sits. He holds up the finger

Kevin 'Cos of my finger.
Maggie Can't you use the other hand?

She sits next to him and opens her coat and he cuddles inside and the coat goes round him so that only her head and their legs are visible—and the legs intertwine

Miriam and Dennis come out of the kitchen

Miriam hovers at the counter as Dennis moves to the doorway to look for Bob but sees the intertwined couple under the fur coat, jerks to a halt and stares— and then goes back to Miriam

Dennis I can't see him anywhere—I suppose we'll just have to tell her.
Miriam But it's all so unfair.
Dennis Put yourself in her place, old love. Imaging sitting here, waiting for Rog to turn up, and all the time he's off somewhere doing—you know ...
Miriam Doing what?
Dennis You know ...
Miriam No I don't know, Dennis, tell me.
Dennis Doing *naughties*.
Miriam (*with her bright smile*) But how can I imagine it because Roger isn't like that, is he Dennis?
Dennis No I'm not saying he is like that, old love.
Miriam Of course you're not saying it because you'd have no reason to say it, would you? Would you Dennis? (*She beams up at him*)

Roger bustles out of the changing-rooms with an armful of pads which he takes straight out to the verandah

Roger All right, Mim, okay? All right Dennis? Super ... (*He deposits the pads on the verandah*) All right, everyone? Jolly good, super ... (*He catches sight of the heaving mass of fur coat, averts his eyes and moves quickly inside again to the changing-rooms*)

Miriam Roger, there's something ...

Roger exits to the changing-rooms

Dennis takes Miriam's arms in his masculine grip

Dennis (*moving out to the verandah*) I'll talk to Virginia, you talk to Roger.

Sharon puts her head round the corner of the pavilion, sees everyone there, and tearfully goes back out of sight. Roger bustles out of the changing-rooms with an armful of stumps. He starts to go straight out with them

Miriam Roger ...

The telephone rings. Roger takes it up cheerfully

Roger (*on the phone*) Good afternoon, this is your captain speaking ... Yes Jeremy, old son, what's the problem? (*His face drops as he listens*)

Miriam goes behind the drinks bar, rearranging things to steady her nerves. Dennis moves to sit next to Ginnie, who becomes aware of him and raises her eyes from her book

Dennis Good book?

Ginnie I try to read one a year: it does so broaden the mind, don't you agree?

Dennis (*taking her hand and patting it paternally*) I know this, Virginia: you're a damn fine woman.

Ginnie What *is* it about me today?

Dennis (*sighing*) I could cry, you know that, Virginia?

Ginnie Dennis ...

Dennis Some men. I dunno.

Alex enters from the changing-rooms, in immaculate whites, and carrying a bat and old ball. He moves out on to the grass. Sharon peers round the corner and moves to him

Alex is more intent on bouncing the ball on the bat than on the following conversation

Sharon Have you got the keys of the car? I want to fetch something.

Alex Now look here, don't go touching any of my switches, will you? (*He gives her the keys*)

Sharon Alex.

Alex Yes?

Sharon I feel ever so uncomfortable.

Alex Well, go for a walk.

Sharon I don't know what to *say* ...

Alex You don't have to say anything, do you? All you have to do is watch *me*. That's why you wanted to come, isn't it? To watch me. Okay—so a lot of 'em aren't your type—you'll just have to do your best, won't you? A lot of 'em aren't my type either but I have to put up with 'em, don't I? Democracy and all that crap. Now look—I've got to get in a spot of practice—enjoy yourself—go and make a daisy chain or something. (*He moves away*)

Sharon (*faintly*) But I want to go home ...

Sharon disappears back round the corner.

Ginnie slowly looks up from her book. It has dawned

Ginnie Dennis ...

Dennis Yes, Virginia?

Ginnie Which particular man did you have in mind?
Alex I say, Dennis ...
Dennis Yes, Alex, old man?
Alex Bit of a knock?

He knocks the ball to Dennis, who catches it and moves to him

Dennis Just going to say the same thing.

Dennis and Alex start to move off

(*with a nudge*) Where d'you meet this one?
Alex She's a gogo dancer at the disco.
Dennis Dirty devil.
Alex I tell you, I can hardly keep my eyes open. Mind you, thick as a plank ...

Alex and Dennis exit to the pitch

Roger slowly replaces the receiver

Roger She's having a baby.
Miriam Oh—super.
Roger What are you talking about, super—she was supposed to be having it tomorrow—he *promised* me. I'm all right for Saturday, he said, she's due to deliver on the Sunday. It's these bloody doctors. They'll do anything so they can go off yachting for the week-end. (*He stares at the team list*) What am I going to do, I'm down to ten again.
Miriam Nine.
Roger What?
Miriam Roger ...
Roger Miriam! *Please.* (*He stares intently at the board*)

Kevin and Maggie change positions so that she is now sitting on his lap, still swamping him in the fur coat

Kevin I'm never gonna play again.
Maggie Yes you are.
Kevin No I'm not.
Maggie Yes you are, it keeps your little body in trim.
Ginnie (*looking up from her book, frowning*) What's he on about, d'you know?
Maggie He's been dropped.
Ginnie Dennis?
Maggie My little Kevin.
Kevin (*muffled under the coat*) My mind is made up. I'll never play for this lot again, not if they got down on their knees and begged me.

Roger is seized by a brilliant idea. He dashes out on to the verandah

Roger Where's Kevin?
Kevin I'm down here.
Roger (*peering*) Where?
Kevin Under this lot.

Maggie And he's not bloody umpiring.
Roger Kev—how would you feel—about going in at number seven?

Instantly Kevin is on his feet, sending Maggie sprawling to the grass

Kevin I'll only do it if I can have a bowl.
Roger What we need is a ruling. Miriam!
Miriam (*hurrying out*) Yes, darling?
Roger Lords.
Miriam Lord who darling?
Roger Not Lord—Lordzzz—M.C.C.—phone number.
Miriam What about it?
Roger I want it, come along woman, chop chop.
Miriam It's on the board, darling, you wrote it down last year, don't you
   remember, when that wicket-keeper chappie turned up covered in plaster-
   of-paris and they said he'd broken his neck and you said you didn't believe
   them so you phoned up for a ruling and there was only that man from
   Securicor there and he referred you to Bart's ...

*Roger hurries inside during the above and examines the phone numbers jotted
down on the notice-board*

Kevin (*moving to the steps*) I've been thinking, Rog—what I need is something
   to harden it up.
Maggie Harden what up?
Kevin My blister.
Roger Miriam!
Miriam Yes, darling?
Roger Something to harden a blister—chop chop.
Miriam Please don't ...
Roger Miriam, *please.*
Maggie Surgical spirit.
Roger (*clicking his finger, pointing to Miriam*) Super.
Miriam We haven't got any.
Roger Well, come on then, woman, you were a boy scout, weren't you?
   Improvize.
Ginnie Keep dipping it into a bowl of rice.
Kevin Eh?
Ginnie That's what Japanese wrestlers do, isn't it?
Miriam Meths!
Roger What?
Miriam Methylated spirits.
Roger Are you sure?
Kevin Well, I'm not.
Maggie Fire-eaters use it and they don't get blisters, do they?
Ginnie Certainly the fire-eaters *I* know don't.
Roger Right. Where is it?
Miriam In the primus tin in the boot.

Roger digs out the car keys and tosses them to Miriam

Roger Off you go then, off you go ...
Miriam Roger ...
Roger (*dialling*) Miriam—*please.*

Miriam begins to move away

(*calling*) Love you, okay, fair enough?

Miriam moves off round the corner as Maggie attempts to help the unwilling Kevin to take off the plaster

Maggie (*as Miriam passes them*) Hasn't he got lovely skin?
Miriam Oh—yes—lovely.

Miriam exits, as Dennis and Alex enter. Alex is holding up the cricket ball

Alex Bloody thing's gone square.
Dennis Where are those new ones I got? Trade less ten.
Ginnie Dennis...
Dennis Yes old love?
Ginnie What were you talking about?
Dennis Shan't be a jiffy.
Kevin Done it! (*He triumphantly holds up the plaster*)

Miriam hurries in with a large bottle of meths

Miriam (*to Alex breathlessly*) She's sitting in the car.
Alex She's not messing about with my switches, I trust?
Miriam No actually—she's crying.
Kevin (*referring to the bottle*) What am I supposed to do with it?
Maggie Dab it on—here.
Kevin I'll do it. (*He tentatively puts the bottle against the injured finger*)
Ginnie Dennis—if you've got something to say to me, say it.

Miriam cannot stand what she fears Dennis might say—so she grabs Kevin's hand and the bottle

Miriam Here, let Mim help you, there's a brave little soldier.
Alex What d'you mean, crying? What's she crying about?

Roger bangs the phone down and dials again

Roger Engaged—how can they be engaged?
Maggie Perhaps there's a blister epidemic.
Roger In my opinion—they'll say you can bowl—as long as you don't use an artificial aid—like a plaster.
Kevin (*flatly*) Fantastic.
Roger That being the case—(*he beams*)—we're back to eleven.
Miriam No Roger—ten.
Roger Ten what?
Miriam Ten men, Roger.
Roger (*pointing to the board*) I've just counted 'em.
Miriam But it's—(*hissing*)—Bob.
Ginnie (*to Dennis*) What about Bob?

Dennis He isn't here.
Roger What are you talking about?

*Bob comes round the corner, coat over sleeve, grinning affably. He has had
a few scotches*

Roger Bob, old chap!
Bob Hello Roger, captain, etcetera. (*He beams, salutes*)
Roger What would you say—to number four?

*Bob gives a big thumbs-up and wink all round. He has not yet seen that Ginnie
is there*

Bob Triffic. I would also say this—I have jus' been to the pub, the saloon
 bar of which contained our opposition—most of them this high—(*indicates
 eight feet tall*)—an' this wide—(*indicates the same width*)—an' all of them
 drinking Bloody Mary's—with real blood. (*Again he gives the big thumbs-
 up and wink—but this time he sees Ginnie and his face drops violently*)
Ginnie Hello, darling.
Bob Oh my God. (*He staggers into the pavilion*)
Ginnie He's drunk.
Miriam (*brightly*) I expect he's been drinking.
Ginnie Why is he *drunk*?
Miriam I don't know, I don't know. (*She hurries inside*)

The following lines are spoken quickly, overlapping

Roger (*into the phone*) Hello, M.C.C.? My name is Roger Dervish, you don't
 know me but I know you and the thing is I've got a bit of a query—
Kevin —I can't get it out!—
Roger —what I need is a ruling—
Kevin —it's stuck! The bloody thing's stuck!

*Kevin stands and holds the bottle to show that it is stuck on the end of his finger.
Maggie moves to help Kevin try to pull it off. Ginnie tries to persuade Dennis
to tell her what is going on. Bob weaves around inside the pavilion. Miriam moves
to Roger to try to talk to him, but he puts his hand to his ear, nodding into the
telephone, his back to everyone else*

All this happens at once, and calypso music swells up, as—

the CURTAIN *falls*

ACT II

The same. About 5.30 p.m.

As the CURTAIN *rises we hear the sound of a ball firmly struck by bat. Roger and Dennis are applauding*

Tea has been taken and Miriam and Maggie are clearing up the pavilion. There are the odd cup and saucer and plate outside on the grass. Maggie still wears her fur coat and moves at her unhurried pace. Miriam has removed her hair bandeau but now wears an apron and large yellow plastic gloves. She is looking decidedly tetchy. Ginnie is stretched out on her lounger. She is now in a bikini and has a lint-pad over her nose in case of sunburn. We sense she hasn't moved for hours. She is reading her book but is increasingly aware that the sun is going down behind the pavilion. Bob is trailing out of the changing rooms, wearing pads, box, etc., ready to go into bat. He is wearing clip-on Polaroid lenses over his glasses. The lenses are in the "up" position so that they stick out like a visor. He carries a glass to the bar and replenishes it with soda from the syphon. He is looking decidedly bilious and shifty by turn. Dennis—near the scoreboard— is not at all confident. He still wears his coat over whites, has a cigarette in his mouth. Roger, in cricket gear and cap that makes him look even more boyish, is at the scorer's seat. He is totally absorbed in the game. His eyes seldom leave the field: his body is alive with the agony and the ecstasy

The scoreboard shows that their opponents scored 137. Their score presently stands at 17 for 1, last man 6. The team bag lies on the grass. It contains a jumble of pads, gloves, bats, etc. The action is punctuated by noises from the field and applause, etc., from the vicinity of the pavilion: not too much applause, since the only onlookers will be the players and a few friends and relatives

Roger (*jiggling his feet with pleasure*) Twenty up!

Dennis puts up the 20 on the scoreboard

Well run! Good shot, Brian! (*To Dennis*) Got a fag, Dennis, I've given up.

Dennis gives Roger a cigarette and lights it for him. Bob moves slowly across to peep through at Ginnie. He looks even more miserable on seeing her. He rubs his stomach, and turns to see Miriam looking at him—not without satisfaction

Miriam You look terrible.
Bob I only had three little ones, you know, Mim.
Miriam For medicinal purposes, of course. Oh no—silly me—it's Ginnie who's ill, isn't it?
Bob You don't think I've got an ulcer starting, do you?
Miriam I don't know what to think about you, Bob, really I don't. Frankly— I just don't understand you. (*She takes a trayful of crockery from Maggie. Brightly*) Thank you so much.

Miriam goes into the kitchen where she bangs around somewhat during the following

Maggie I think she's upset.

Bob It's me. I've done it all wrong again.

Maggie No, it's the teas. Them not being here on time. Kevin's exactly the same. If you're not sitting down salivating dead on the dot he goes all sulky.

Bob I only had three, you know, three little whiskies.

Maggie When my Kev has a few drinks he has a lie-down. That's what you should've done instead of all that running about out there.

Ginnie moves the lounger a little more into the sun

Bob I can't drink, y'see. Something to do with my metabolic rate of exchange. Hey—what about my bowling, eh? Talk about a knife through butter. I *had* to play, didn't I? (*He peers round at Ginnie*)

More runs are being scored, and Roger and Dennis applaud

Maggie What's happening?

Bob She's moving her chair.

Maggie Is that why they're clapping?

Bob Eh? Oh, no, they're running. Look at the way he runs.

Maggie Who?

Bob That Alex. I don't know what they see in him, I'm sure he wears mascara.

Maggie Is his girl-friend out there?

Bob Can't see her. I'm next man in, you know.

Maggie Gerraway, I thought you were going skateboarding. (*She sits on a stool and rolls herself a cigarette*)

Bob sighs heavily

Go and give her a cuddle, go on.

Bob Who?

Maggie Your wife, who d'you think?

Bob (*glumly*) She hates me.

Maggie 'Course she doesn't.

Bob They all hate me, sooner or later. I've been married before, you know.

Maggie I did hear, yes.

Bob Yes. What's she been saying about me?

Maggie Who?

Bob (*jerking his thumb towards kitchen*) Madam Bountiful.

Maggie She told me you'd been married before, what's so terrible about that?

Bob (*glowering, but rubbing his stomach*) I am ill, I know I am.

Maggie Men. You're ill, you need rest. A woman's ill, she needs exercise.

A run is scored

Bob He's a solicitor. That Alex. Daddy's practice, surprise surprise.

Maggie Kevin doesn't like him either.

Bob I'm not saying I don't like him, I'm just saying he makes me sick.

*Ginnie, again irritably repositioning her lounger, sees Bob looking. He "waves",
puts on a smile*

Oh Gawd, why did I have to leave that bag behind? You know why she's
here, don't you? Checking up on me.

Maggie Then she must have a reason, mustn't she, my old fruit?

*Miriam comes out of the kitchen. She beams at Maggie, pointedly ignores
Bob, and goes out to speak to Roger. She has clearly been brooding on this*

Miriam I don't like having to say this Roger but I'm going to say it neverthe-
less: I really am most awfully cross.

Roger's eyes never leave the play

Roger Who is?

Miriam A quarter-to-five you said, I distinctly heard you, a quarter-to-five,
instead of which it was half-past-four which meant I was totally unprepared
and made to look a complete fool and no-one seemed to give a tuppenny
whatsit—it just isn't fair, Roger.

Roger *("patiently")* You asked me what time we wanted tea, and the way
things were going I said about quarter to because *I* didn't know Bob was
going to bowl like that, did I? Blame him, not me.

A great cry of "Howzat?" goes up

Mirimam It's the same every week, I do my best to make things nice and ...

Dennis That blackie's throwing 'em down a bit, isn't he?

Roger I'll say—what? (*He puffs out his cheeks*) Miriam, much as I know you'd
like me to, I cannot control this game to accommodate the taking of your
refreshments. Rather ... (*He winces at a fast ball*) Crikey look at that.
Rather, the other way about. What's he signalling? No ball, right, fair
enough, 'bout bloody time.

*Roger acknowledges the umpire, ignoring Miriam who glares down at him in
impotent rage*

Miriam (*all she can manage*) Well, you should have *said* something. (*She starts
to move away then stops*) You should, you should have said something. (*She
moves on to the steps*)

Roger (*referring to the umpire*) Short-sighted pillock.

*Miriam, on the steps, turns quickly, misconstruing, but Roger is staring out at
the pitch. She moves quickly inside, and sees Bob*

Miriam It just isn't fair—not only do you ruin my catering arrangements but
you will involve other people in your—in your ...

Bob It isn't what you ...

Miriam I'm sorry, I don't wish to talk about it. (*She stalks regally to the
kitchen. To Maggie, on the way*) No, it's all right, thank you I can manage.

Miriam exits to the kitchen

Maggie Oo-er. I hate washing-up, don't you? You know what I say—here
today, here tomorrow.

Bob It isn't what you think.

Maggie drifts out on to the steps, wiping her nose with a tissue

> *Sharon puts her head round the corner—but on seeing everyone, ducks back out of sight before Maggie can get rid of the tissue and speak to her. Maggie goes off round the corner after her*

Bob steps out into the sunlight, pulling down the visor so that his glasses are covered

(*Brightly*) All right love?

Ginnie lowers her book and looks up at him

Ginnie Why are you avoiding me?
Bob Me? (*He "laughs"*) Just concentrating, that's all.
Ginnie You're doing it now: hiding behind those silly glasses.
Bob I happen to have bad eyes.
Ginnie Oh I see, you're ill again.
Bob I did not say I was ill, I said I had bad eyes.

Bob tries to make it all sound like pleasant chit-chat for the benefit of Dennis, who is grinning at him, aware that he is getting stick

Ginnie You've always got something wrong with you.
Bob That is not true: I happen to have bad eyes.
Ginnie And a bad stomach.
Bob And a bad stomach.
Ginnie Your legs aren't up to much either.
Bob Thank you darling, thankyousomuch.

> *Miriam comes out of the kitchen to continue busying around, in perverse pleasure at having no assistance*

Bob eases himself away towards Roger and Dennis

Dennis How you feeling, old boy?
Bob I had *three* whiskies, that's all.
Dennis No, I mean—(*he mimes a shot*)—confident?
Bob (*"smugly"*) I'm all right, thankyouverymuch.
Dennis (*with a nudge*) Bit of a shock the old woman turning up though, eh? (*Putting his finger to his lips*) Mim's the word, eh?
Bob You know, Dennis: underneath that insensitive exterior of yours, you're really quite insensitive, aren't you?
Dennis (*grinning*) I know you're a bit of an all-rounder but I don't know how you concentrate, old man, really I don't. Well played, Alex, good shot! Still. What does it all come down to in the end? Sex. Is it worth it? Can it really be worth it? (*He smirks*)

Bob glowers a moment, then moves forward

Bob Oh look ...

Dennis (*moving to him*) What?
Bob There's that old man with the black dog.
Dennis Where?
Bob There.
Dennis I can't see him.
Bob He's gone. How very peculiar.
Dennis Well I didn't see him.

Dennis remains staring out as Bob moves away

Bob Yes, you're right: probably wasn't him at all.
Roger Who?
Dennis No-one.
Bob That old man with the black dog Dennis reckons brings him bad luck.
(*Pointing suddenly*) Oh look, there he is, going behind that tree. You don't
think he's a flasher as well, do you? They do say if you stand behind that
tree you can flash over seven counties. Good shot!

Maggie enters

Maggie She's sitting in the car.
Bob Oh really?
Maggie She says she prefers it.

*Maggie sits on the steps and reads a copy of the "Socialist Worker", as Dennis
stares out at the pitch and Bob rubs his stomach*

Ginnie Your stomach playing you up again, is it?
Bob Me? No ...
Ginnie That means you're up to something. What are you up to?
Bob (*sighing*) Virginia ...
Ginnie Actually, I don't give a pair of knickers *what* you're up to and you're
in my sun, thankyousomuch darling.
Bob Sorry.
Ginnie But since you mention it there's something going on and I don't like
it.

Bob moves to sit close to her

Bob All right—what? What can be going on?
Ginnie People being nice to me, that's what I mean, people like her—(*meaning
Miriam*)—she's never nice to me.
Bob *Ginnie.*
Ginnie You think I don't know when you're up to something—you're collud-
ing, aren't you?
Bob Who is?
Ginnie All of you. (*It suddenly dawns*) Why weren't you here when I tele-
phoned?
Bob Me?

*Suddenly there is a great shout from the field—a wicket has gone down. The
men slump*

Oh Christ ... (*A moment, then, all-action as he fumbles around, getting his batting gear together—bat, gloves, hoiks up his protective box, still with the fag stuck out of his mouth and the sunglasses on*)

Dennis and Roger applaud the unseen player leaving the field

Roger Well played Brian bad luck—oh Gawd, he's upset. Go and get those pads off him, Dennis, before he throws 'em in the river again.

Dennis moves off quickly

Bob prepares to go out to bat, remembers the cigarette and crushes it underfoot, remembers his Polaroid attachment, which he cannot take off because of his clumsy gloves. He sees Ginnie holding her hand out and gives her his glasses. She removes the attachment and returns the glasses to him

(*Slapping*) Off you go then, Bob, chop chop.
Ginnie Yes—have a *lovely* time, darling—and it had better not be what I think it is—all right?

There is scattered applause as Bob exits, and Kevin enters hurriedly from the wickets in his cricket gear but wearing a white umpire's coat about ten sizes too large

Maggie stands and applauds Kevin wildly

Kevin You don't have to clap me, you silly great haystack. (*To Roger*) I've had enough of that, Rog.

Roger alters the board to read: 29 for 2, last man 10, Maggie sits on the steps

Roger Err—right—fair enough. Tell Arnold to take over, he's only mucking about with his kids.
Kevin I'm lucky to be alive, I'm telling you.
Maggie You look really nice in white, Kev: if your little legs had been a bit longer you would have made a lovely bride.
Kevin (*moving off, waving the coat*) Arnold!

Kevin exits. Dennis enters, clutching a pair of pads, gloves, a bat—and looking somewhat shaken

Dennis He says it's hell out there. (*He goes inside the pavilion, passing Miriam but not seeing her, on his way into the changing-rooms*)

Dennis exits

Ginnie Dear God, let him have a decent innings.

Miriam enters

Maggie Are you keen on cricket then?
Ginnie Good God no, dearie: I want him out of my way so I can finish this rotten book.

Miriam moves to stand in the doorway

Miriam I don't know if I prefer Rog to have a good innings or a bad one.

If it's a good one, he re-lives it in bed, shot by shot, and if it's a bad one he actually replays the shots until he gets it right. He can make a really good innings last all winter.

Kevin enters

Roger and Kevin stare intently at the play. Bob is about to face his first ball. There is a great shout of "Howzat?" Roger and Kevin wince

Dennis comes dashing out, and pad on, one pad off, to stare

The decision goes in Bob's favour. Kevin and Roger heave sighs of relief

Dennis trails back into the changing-room

Maggie (*to Kevin*) Those trousers are too long—come here ... (*She rises, hoiking Kevin's trousers up, almost lifting him off his feet*)
Kevin Get off me, woman!

She cuddles him from behind

Maggie Ooo he's trembling, d'you know that, the whole of his little body is trembling it is.

There is some applause and Kevin and Roger join in gratefully as Miriam—suddenly remembering her bad mood—addresses no-one in particular

Miriam No it's all right thankyou, I can manage. (*She goes to take the cloth off the table*)
Kevin Well played, Robert! That's him off the mark. He'll be pleased, and I am not trembling—I am alive with nervous anticipation.
Maggie Oo-er!
Roger Thirty up!

Kevin frees himself from Maggie and moves to alter the board

Maggie Look at the muscles on that black one.
Ginnie (*lowering her glasses*) Which black one?
Maggie The one who's sulking.
Kevin He's not walking away because he's sulking, he's walking away to begin his nine hundred yard run-up, you dozy great cow.

Dennis enters from the changing-rooms, with pads on and carrying his bat

Miriam Ah, Dennis, I wonder if you'd be so kind as to help me fold this cloth?

Dennis props his bat against the wall

Dennis It would be—*une plaisir.*

He takes two corners of the large cloth and they fold it neatly between them, moving backwards and forwards—a movement that Dennis contrives to turn into a little dance

Miriam (*stiffly*) I'm sorry about the teas not being quite up to scratch, you see Roger distinctly told me a quarter to and when everyone came waltzing in here at half past—you know, it just isn't fair, Dennis.

Dennis Miriam my love—the tea—was as ever—a picture.

Miriam Thankyouverymuch Dennis, but that simply isn't true. There are standards, you see.

Dennis Miriam: you are one hundred and one per cent. Believe me.

At this moment they are close together, holding the cloth between them, chest to chest, and Dennis is moving her backwards in the little dance—and Maggie enters the pavilion

Maggie I wondered if you needed a hand.

Maggie does an exaggerated little copy of their steps: and again Miriam is aware of being "caught"

Dennis We were just discussing the late string quartets of Ludwig Van Beethoven.

Maggie Oh yeah?

Maggie grins and moves outside "laughing" like the four opening notes of Beethoven's fifth symphony and Miriam smiles at Dennis, indicating he is dismissed. Dennis takes up his bat and sits on the table, staring anxiously out at the game

Miriam goes off to the kitchen

Kevin moves over next to Roger and both pairs of eyes remain glued on the game

Kevin If I was a medical man, which I very nearly could have been, I'd give that bowler a saliva test, he's twice as fast as he was last year.

Roger We've got to beat 'em, you know, Kev. It's not just the game, it's a matter of principle. I hate 'em, I *hate* 'em.

Applause

Four to Alex—sooo-per. Put it up will you, Kev, you know how these solicitors like things in writing.

Kevin (*altering the board*) I tell you: they've really got it in for us. I was terrified out there, and I was only umpiring. What they said to me when I gave that "Not Out" is nobody's business. That's why I had to come in, me nerves wouldn't stand it.

Sharon appears, unnoticed, round the corner. Actually, she is getting desperate for a pee but just cannot face making a personal appearance. She goes back out of sight again

Ginnie casts a final despairing look at the sky, then stands to collect up her things

Ginnie That's it then: good-bye sun.

Ginnie goes inside and exits into the changing-rooms, carrying her bag

Kevin You know what that one in the red cap said to me?

Roger Which one in the red cap?

Kevin The one in the red cap.

Roger What about him?

Kevin You know what he said to me? "Just don't go down any dark alleys on your way home tonight," he says. *Me.* "Listen brother," I says, "I'm one of you, I'm a member of the *Party.*"

Maggie You do, Kev, you look really nice in white, I think I'm falling in love with you.

Maggie "coyly" hides her face behind her newspaper. Kevin grins and moves to her

Kevin You wouldn't let 'em beat me up down an alley, would you Mag?
Maggie 'Course I wouldn't.
Kevin I couldn't 'arf do with a cuddle.
Maggie Come here, then.

She opens her arms and he lies on the steps and puts his head in her lap; she strokes his brow

Better?
Dennis (*suddenly*) You haven't seen an old man with a black dog, have you by any chance?

Miriam enters from the kitchen with a broom

She brushes the floor, and Dennis remains sitting on the table, raising his padded legs for her to sweep under

Anyway, I've found the secret, you know.

Miriam sweeps irritably, not looking at him

Miriam Oh really?
Dennis Came to me in a flash. I should've been putting my left pad on first. I should've remembered that time I scored eighty-seven not out against Finchley Grammar School.
Miriam Oh yes?
Dennis The past five innings I haven't done too well, right? Because I was putting my right pad on first, not my left, right? *Right.*

Miriam moves irritably to the steps

Miriam I wonder if someone would like to give me a hand? Thankyousomuch.

Maggie grimaces, throws down her paper, kisses the top of Kevin's head and goes inside

Thankyousomuch.

Miriam bustles into the kitchen, and Maggie slopes in after her

Dennis moves to the steps

Dennis Brian says it's hell out there.
Kevin They hate us after what we did to 'em last year.
Dennis You did to 'em—you and ·Bob.
Kevin I would've done 'em this year an' all if it hadn't been for my finger. Still. Bob sorted 'em out. I mean. Considering he could hardly stand up. Doing all right with the bat an' all, isn't he?

Dennis Oh yes—a very fine all-rounder in every sense of the word is friend Roberto.

Suddenly they both wince and almost take evasive action and Kevin rises, hands thrust deep into the pockets of his baggy trousers

Kevin Cor, look at that, they're only trying to kill him. Bloody hell. (*A moment*) You're in next, aren't you? (*He sucks in air*) He'll still be fresh. Mind you—now you've put your pads on the right way round, he's got no chance.

Dennis I'll say—what!

Dennis thrashes his bat around as Kevin moves to resume sitting on the steps

Maggie comes out of the kitchen, pouts a big kiss at Kevin and goes back inside

Dennis moves to sit next to Kevin, who amuses himself by feeding Dennis' well-known frustrations

Fine looking woman, your wife.

Kevin She loves me y'know, silly cow.

Dennis They do *cling*, don't they?

Kevin We had a really smashing time last night. I made a really triffic *quiche lorraine* and she dug a tree out of the garden. It was really triffic, know what I mean, really nice. She's being so reasonable I think I'll tell her I'll go ahead with this adoption thing. She can't have one, you know. Well—anything to keep the silly cow happy. It'll take two years to go through, by which time I'll probably have left her, anyway.

Dennis You've only just got married.

Kevin It's the sex, isn't it? Sex-mad she is. I can't trust her y'see, Dennis—not with anyone. Not a soul. Mind you, it's the only thing she's any good at. That and building. Lays a very nifty brick, I'll give her that. I'm gonna get her to build herself a little flat down in the basement. With a communicating door so I can send down the food and she can come up for the sex. You think *she's* big, you should see her sister—a giant she is, fantastic.

A four is scored: applause

Miriam enters from the kitchen

Roger Forty up!

Kevin moves quickly over to change the board

I think we've got the buggers, I can feel it! (*He rubs his hands together gleefully*)

Ginnie enters from the changing-rooms, now wearing her dress again. She sees Miriam

Ginnie I've just done my nails but if there's anything I can do?

Miriam Thankyousomuch Virginia, but we'll manage somehow, truly we will.

Ginnie goes outside to sit on her lounger

Maggie enters from the kitchen

Maggie D'you want this table folded up?
Miriam (*after staring at her for a moment*) Excuse me one moment, will you?

Miriam goes outside and directly to Roger. Maggie folds the table and props it back against the wall, then drifts across to throw some darts

Roger darling, I know you think I'm making an awful fuss, but I don't think you realize just how important these things are to me.

Roger does not take his eyes from the game once

Roger 'Course I do.
Miriam No, you don't—you see, Roger, that's the awful thing, after all these years, you don't.

During the following Dennis sees Maggie alone. Kevin sits in the canvas chair, watching the game intently. Dennis pulls out his wallet and "casually" drifts inside

Roger Don't what?
Miriam What I'm saying, Roger, is that we really must come to some sort of better arrangement *vis-à-vis* the taking of tea. It simply isn't good enough to expect me to . . .
Roger Miriam . . .
Miriam Yes, darling?
Roger Shut up.
Miriam Roger, I . . .
Roger Shut up shut up shut up!

Miriam recoils in horror, then tries to hold a bright smile as though nothing has happened, and moves slowly away from him

Miriam, love you but we're trying to win a game, all right, okay, fair enough?

Miriam holds her fixed smile as she goes into the pavilion

Miriam Yes, fine, super, thankyousomuch.

Miriam goes quickly into the kitchen

Dennis moves up close behind Maggie as she throws the darts, and holds up his business card

Dennis If ever you need a carpet, just give me a tinkle.

Maggie takes the card. He holds her hand, gives her his sincere look and pats her hand

Wholesale definitely. Probably—not definitely mind, but probably—a bit more. (*Again he pats the hand*) Okay?
Maggie You don't 'arf turn me on, Dennis. Spiritually I mean.

Maggie grinds her behind into Dennis. Actually, he makes her feel sick. She drifts out on to the verandah

I'll just pop round and see how she is.

Maggie goes round to the car-park exit, patting Kevin's head as she goes

Dennis follows Maggie out on to the verandah, and leers after her. Kevin sees him doing so, and stares at him

Dennis I was just saying to Maggie—if ever you need anything—just pop round to the shop.

Miriam enters and fusses around behind the tea counter

Kevin Yes, we might do that when she's finished knocking the two sitting-rooms together. At least I'll send her round, can't stand shopping myself.

Dennis Yes, well, anyway, I'll look after her—you know me, good old Uncle Dennis.

Ginnie makes her mind up and goes inside to speak to Miriam

Ginnie I said, do you want some help?

Miriam No thanks, it's not compulsory you know, really.

Ginnie Well you're going to get some whether you want it or not.

Miriam Sorry?

Ginnie I'm going to help you stop worrying—about me and Bob and things that don't bloodywell concern you because whatever you're thinking you've got it wrong. Sorry, Miriam, but there's no trouble, no trouble at all. So instead of worrying about us, why don't you worry about—Dorking?

Miriam Dorking? I don't know Dorking.

Ginnie No dearie: but Roger does. (*With a satisfied smile*) Ask "the chaps". (*She goes outside to resume sitting*)

Miriam stares

Maggie enters

Maggie She's just sitting in the car, biting her little nails.

Ginnie Perhaps she collects car numbers.

Maggie She's just shy, that's all. (*She sits on the steps*) She's been there all afternoon. Well, apart from teatime, and then only for five minutes. *He* never said a word to her.

Kevin Who?

Maggie Your friend Alex. He ignores her. All the way through tea, not a dickey.

Kevin He's the same with all of 'em, never says a word.

Maggie I'm sure she'd come round here if we could persuade her somehow.

Ginnie Well I'll tell you what, dearie—she seemed awfully partial to Miriam's veal and ham pie. Why don't you lead a trail of it round the corner, like they do with squirrels.

Dennis Mind you. The sort they *are*.

Kevin Squirrels?

Dennis Alex's bits of stuff. I mean—not exactly too much going on up here (*He taps his forehead*) is there, any of them.

Maggie You like a woman to be intelligent, do you, Den?

Dennis Well I like 'em to have *something* up here. I mean, there's more to life than just the body, isn't there?

Maggie clicks her tongue and gives him a pseudo-sexy wink

What do you say, Kev?

Kevin All I've ever asked of a woman is that she devotes her entire life to me.

Maggie The terrible thing is, he means it. And the even more terrible thing is, I'm prepared to do it.

Dennis Come on now—surely you rebel sometimes?

Maggie True: sometimes I won't eat his egg custard.

Kevin Lovely, my egg custard.

Dennis Be honest, girls, you like to be dominated. True or false?

Maggie Oh true, ever so true. You're ever so perceptive, Dennis, you really are.

Miriam comes out on to the verandah, beams around and starts collecting up the cups and saucers from the grass

Miriam Well now—how's it going, everyone?

Maggie It's not as invigorating as stock-car racing, is it?

Miriam Sorry?

Maggie What happens when it rains?

Miriam Ah! Well now—when it rains, they sulk and I make endless cups of tea, isn't that right, Kevin?

Kevin True, very true.

Miriam Endless cups of tea that become endless glasses of pale ale that become endless stories of triumphs past. (*She bends close to the seated Kevin*) Does Dorking mean anything to you?

Kevin Not a lot, no.

Dennis Miriam's teas are an art form, that's what I say.

Roger (*rising*) Good God, that's not bowling, the man's a chucker!

Dennis stares fearfully out at the wicket, then quietly slips out to the car-park

Miriam!

Miriam Yes, darling.

Roger I'm parched, get me a soft drink of some sort, will you?

Miriam Yes, darling.

Roger (*licking his lips exaggeratedly*) Come along then woman, chop chop.

The telephone starts to ring

And stop that ringing!

Miriam fumbles her way inside with the cups and saucers. Maggie moves to the phone and takes it up

Maggie Hang on.

Maggie holds out the receiver for Miriam who is still juggling with the crockery

Ginnie Funny thing about men: as soon as they stop loving you they expect you to become super-efficient.

Maggie Funny thing about my Kev is, he can never resist arguing with a Jehovah's Witness.

Miriam (*into the phone*) Hello? ... Oh hello, Shirley, yes he is, just a minute ... (*She puts down the phone and hurries outside to call*) Dennis? (*She cannot see him so she hurries back to take up the phone and jots down a message*) He seems to have disappeared ... Yes of course I will ...

Ginnie How did you two meet?

Maggie I won him in a raffle.

Kevin First prize was a week-end in Bognor.

Maggie He's my first and only love, aren't you? (*She embraces Kevin fondly*)

Kevin Gerroff.

Ginnie Oh really? I'd been with twelve men before I met Bob. He made it twelve and a half.

Dennis enters, self-consciously wearing a protective helmet with visor

Miriam replaces the receiver and hurries outside, sees Dennis, and moves to him

Miriam Shirley just telephoned.

Dennis Oh, what's happened now?

Miriam She said to tell you she's seen the house—she's still there, as a matter of fact—that it's exactly what she's always wanted but they must have a decision today because there's another young couple after it, so could you please ring her there and go round and have a look at it—there's the number, thankyousomuch.

Miriam gives Dennis the slip of paper and moves inside. Dennis looks up from the paper to see Kevin and Maggie grinning at his helmet

Dennis I'm just testing it for the manager of the sports department, actually.

Maggie Looks like a drink on a stick.

Dennis What's that my lovely?

Maggie I said, that should do the trick.

There is a sudden burst of activity from the field and the men applaud

Roger Fifty up!

Their applause is even more enthusiastic as Dennis alters the board

We've got 'em, we've flippingwell got 'em!

Roger gets up on his chair to see better, as Miriam moves out quickly to him

Miriam Roger ...

Roger Where's my squash?

Miriam Roger, I'm sorry to go on about this, but ...

Roger Miriam. If I was out there, batting to win, and you were in here, sobbing your heart out about your timetable—I would bat and if necessary go on batting all night, even if it meant using a Davey lamp and taking your stupid bloody tea intravenously. Now where's my *squash*? (*He glares down at her from his chair*)

Miriam backs away, shocked, and goes into the pavilion to make a glass of squash, but then changes her mind and hurls darts savagely into the board. Dennis shoves the paper into his pocket

Dennis (*generally*) What a time to phone up. That was Shirley. Still nagging me about a new house. Wouldn't you think she'd be able to make her own decisions, eh? I keep telling her. "Shirley my love—you make the decision—then bring it to me—and I'll tell you where you've gone wrong." Now, I couldn't say fairer than that to the dear old thing, now could I. (*He smiles and starts to take out a cigarette*)

There is a great cry of "Howzat". The men stare—awaiting the umpire's decision and the reaction from the field is enough to indicate that someoné is out. Now it is Dennis' turn to look panicstricken. He jerks himself around, discreetly slipping a false front tooth into a handkerchief, then grabbing up gloves and bat. Roger looks depressed and Kevin moves to change the board, which now reads: 53 for 3, last man 13.

Dennis goes out, a bag of nerves

Roger Good luck Dennis—don't worry old mate—it's only a game ...

Bob enters

Kevin and Roger clap, ad-libbing "well played", etc., but Bob, furious, throws down his bat

Bob (*generally*) Did you see that? The bugger ran me out. One I said, one—but oh no, he has to go for two, doesn't he? Bloody deliberate that was, bloody deliberate.
Ginnie Bob darling ...

She beckons Bob to her, "smiling". He had forgotten about their problem, but now moves to her sheepishly

Bob Sorry about that, love: the man's nothing but a glory-seeker.

Ginnie beckons him to bend so that she can talk into his ear, still with a smile

Ginnie What rotten luck, darling—and it isn't over yet, is it? I still want to know what's been going on, don't I, silly old me?

He looks at her and tries to bluff it out

Bob Virginia, I've just been run out ...
Ginnie Yes of course you have—now toddle off and have someone throw a blanket over you before you catch distemper or something.

A moment, then Bob goes through and into the changing-rooms

Kevin (*sucking in air*) Was a bit dodgy, that second run.
Roger Where's Charles, all padded up is he? (*Looking round*) Oh yes. (*He gives the thumbs-up sign to the unseen Charles*) Happy Charles, okay? Jolly good. (*With a change of tone*) Gawd look at the size of him, he can hardly walk let alone get a run.

Miriam comes outside and sits to watch the game

Maggie (*after a moment*) I don't understand what they get so worked up about.

Ginnie Oh I don't know, it's good for them, it takes their little minds off the nastier side of life.

Maggie What do women have to take their minds off the nastier side of life? I mean, it's all right for them with their football and their cricket and their Friday nights down the pub. But what about us?

Ginnie We've got *them*, surely?

Maggie I thought they *were* the nastier side of life.

Miriam Surely one needs to find oneself a rewarding hobby.

Ginnie Like flower-arranging. Or prostitution.

Maggie I thought about going on the game once.

Ginnie Surely you'd have to do it more than once to make it profitable?

Miriam (*gaily*) I trust you discussed the matter with Kevin?

Maggie Oh, he was all for it: as long as I don't bring my work home with me, he said.

Maggie sits in the canvas chair. There is a great shout from the pitch

Bob trails in from the changing-rooms, now minus pads

Roger and Kevin look horrified. Bob dashes to the door

Bob What's happened?

Roger cannot speak—his head in his hands

Kevin Dennis—first ball.
Bob Not first ball, oh dear.

There is some consolation in all things. Kevin changes the board to read: 53 for 4, last man 0

First ball, poor old Den, oh dear oh dear oh dear. (*He beams, thrusting hands in pockets and jiggling his legs with the sheer pleasure of it*)

Dennis, white-faced, trudges back in

Roger (*calling but wearily*) Good luck, Chas, nice and easy now old mate, plenty of time ...
Kevin Box—where's my bloody box?

Kevin scuttles into the changing-rooms

Dennis Bloody hell skip, I mean—did you see it? I mean—bloody hell, I mean ...

Roger keeps his head in hands as he speaks

Roger I mean—bloody hell, skip—it must've moved about three feet—I mean ...
Roger Don't *worry*. Old mate ... (*But his eyes are glued firmly to the play and he heaves a sigh of relief as the next man survives his first ball*)

Bob Happens to all of us (*beaming*)—some time or other—no-one could have played a ball like that—well—very few of us, anyway.

Dennis That ball moved three feet if it moved an inch.

Bob At least you got out by dint of your own inadequacy: not like me, run out by a bloody ego-maniac.

Roger (*delightedly*) That's Charles off the mark, well played, Charles!

Dennis trudges through into the changing-rooms

Bob grins after him, but then his face drops as he sees Ginnie looking at him. She beckons him with crooked finger. He holds up a hand, indicating "just a minute" and goes across to stare down unnecessarily at the scorebook

Kevin dashes out of the changing-rooms, hoisting up his box

Kevin Pads, pads …

Kevin dashes across to sort out a pair of pads from the team bag and sits in the canvas chair to put them on. Maggie moves to help him, kneeling in front of him and only causing the job to take twice as long

Sharon enters from the car-park, unable to contain herself much longer

Sharon Excuse me …

Miriam Yes, of course, how can I help you?

Sharon I was wondering if I could avail myself of your toilet.

Miriam Sorry?

Sharon The toilet.

Miriam Oh—the toilet. The door on the right. There's a sign up actually.

Sharon Sorry?

Miriam (*enunciating loudly*) There is a sign up on the door.

Everyone watches Sharon as she nervously moves in towards the pavilion doors

Sharon I would have gone before we come out, that's what I usually do, it drives me dad mad—well I call him me dad, but you know—he says why can't you do it before you get all dressed up? I suppose he's right in a way, I mean it does seem daft getting all ready and everything and then having to go to the toilet but my mum's the same, she says it's something to do with a woman's mechanisms. Anyway, I would have gone and normally I'm very good—I mean normally I can last—but he was in such a hurry— not my dad—Alex …

The others stare at her, transfixed

Oh yes—it's through there. Sorry.

Sharon hurries inside, and is about to go into the changing-rooms when Dennis bursts out, face like thunder. He still wears whites, but has his coat and ordinary shoes on. He has a fag in his mouth, is holding the slip of paper, and is digging out a 2p piece

Sharon cowers away at his sudden appearance—and she remains there, unable to get past him as he dials the phone

Roger Flipping heck, he's going like the clappers! Well played Chas, keep it going old mate! Sixty up!

Bob changes the board

Dennis (*pressing in the coin; smarmily*) Oh hello, good afternoon, this is Mister Broadley speaking ... That's right, broadly speaking, yes—I understand you have my good lady with you ... Thankyousomuch. (*A moment, then, with a total change of tone*) Shirley? ... You did that deliberately, didn't you? You willed that ball to swing through the air like that—I could feel it—just so that I'd have to see that stupid rotten house. Well you can forget it, all right, forget it.

Bob, wary of Ginnie, sneaks inside and pours himself a scotch

Roger We are scoring at the rate of four point two an over!
Maggie Lummee!
Dennis (*on the phone*) I'll explain it to you—as simply as I can. I shall need to do that, shan't I, so that you can understand. In fact, I shall use only four words and five syllables—ready? We-are-not-moving.

Sharon is about to go into the changing-rooms

   Bob moves smartly past her and goes inside, slamming the door

Sharon feels even more trapped

Kevin (*to Maggie*) What are you doing?
Maggie I'm doing up your straps.
Kevin Get off, you great fat—I'm not Houdini.

Kevin stands up and waddles away—she has tied both pads together. He sits down and adjusts the pads. Dennis continues his phone call. Sharon tries to indicate that she wants to go into the changing-rooms. Dennis misconstrues, thinks she is waving at him, and flutters fingers at her

Roger Where's my squash?

   Miriam stomps through into the kitchen

Dennis (*on the phone*) Why have I allowed you to look at houses? What a very good question. You see, you can use your brain when you want to. I let you look at houses because I want you to be happy. I let you look at houses because you've done nothing but complain ever since we moved into our new one and I wanted you to go around looking at other places just to see what a lucky girl you are ... No I'm not arguing with you, Shirley, you've already ruined my day ... What? ... No, Shirley, you're not unhappy, you only think you are—now say goodbye to the nice people, explain to them that you're not very bright, and go home.

Dennis puts down the receiver, smiling at Sharon. He strolls outside. Sharon makes to go into the changing-rooms again

   Bob bursts out, still in whites but wearing a jacket. He is smoking a cigarette

Sharon jumps back nervously. Bob vents his anger on her

Bob I reckon it was deliberate, you know. He knew I was in for a big score and he just couldn't stand someone stealing his limelight, that's what I reckon. What do you *see* in him?

Bob goes outside, tries to avoid being seen by Ginnie, but she smiles sweetly and beckons him to her. He moves to her. Sharon tries to get into the changing-room—but the door is jammed. She presses against it helplessly

Ginnie (*"lightly"*) When I phoned, you were with *her*, weren't you?
Bob Ginnie . . .
Ginnie Just yes or no or I'll scream this shed down.
Bob She phoned up: she wanted to see me.
Ginnie I see.
Bob It's not what you . . .
Ginnie No no dearie that's all I wanted to hear. (*She beams*) Now sod off, will you?
Bob Ginnie . . .
Ginnie (*shouting*) Sod off!

She swings her bag violently at Bob. He takes evasive action and goes inside the pavilion. Ginnie sorts out her bottle of Valium

Sharon Excuse me . . .

Bob takes a swig of the whisky and points towards Sharon, who covers back as he advances on her

Bob I blame that thing. (*He points to the phone*) I do, I blame that thing for everything. It only costs tuppence to make someone miserable. Think how much happier we'd all be if we couldn't just pick up one of those and arrange things. (*He mimes using the phone, still advancing on the retreating Sharon*) "Hello, I just happened to be in the area and I wondered if I might pop round for a cuppa coffee, etcetera, etcetera,"—pressing the money in, little heart thumping. I wonder how much of that misplaced passion would survive if you had to put it in writing and stick a stamp on it? Good-bye Heavy Breathing Hello True Romance. Sealed with a loving kiss oh happy days. (*Suddenly*) What do you *see* in him?

Bob glares at Sharon, who dashes fearfully out to the verandah

Maggie Oh. Hello.
Sharon It's quite nice here really, isn't it?

Miriam comes out of the kitchen and sees Bob

Maggie offers Sharon a bag of toffees and they sit next to each other on the steps

Miriam (*to Bob*) You see, Roger and I have nothing to hide . . .
Maggie Wanna toffee?
Sharon Get stuck in me teeth . . .
Miriam And I'll tell you something else. My teas were a complete shambles today because I was on tenterhooks the whole time about you and Virginia . . .

Maggie D'you like cricket?

Miriam I'm sorry, but there it is. (*She goes to the kitchen*)

Bob Miriam—there's more to life than your bloody teas. That clown just ran me out!

Miriam exits into the kitchen as Bob talks

Having "padded up", Kevin has a few practice swings with the bat

Maggie Look at my little Kev. Like a greyhound in the slips. Well, whippet anyway. A lovely little fat whippet. Ooo—I could eat him.

Sharon The woman next door to us bought a dog.

Maggie Oh yeah?

Sharon She was scared of being attacked when she went out at night.

Ginnie There's such a lot of it about, isn't there?

Sharon We think it's a bit funny because she never went out at night anyway. She has to go out at night now though to exercise the dog.

Maggie My Kevin keeps on about getting a dog. I can't have children, you see.

Sharon We had a cat.

Maggie We were going to see the specialist and he suddenly turns round to me and says "Just in case you're disappointed again, how would you like a cocker spaniel?" I could have crowned him.

Sharon His name was Percy.

Maggie Who?

Sharon Our cat. He ran away.

Suddenly Sharon's bladder gets the better of her and she runs into the pavilion and bursts through the changing-room door

Ginnie (*after Sharon has gone*) Percy wasn't the only one it would seem.

Miriam enters from the kitchen. She sees Bob and decides to try another tack. She remains behind the tea counter

Miriam (*brightly*) Bob ...

Bob (*moving to her*) Yes, Miriam old chap?

Miriam You remember we were having a bit of fun and everything and you said something about Rog being a bit of a pushover and we all had a jolly good laugh, it wouldn't be anything to do with Dorking, would it?

Bob Dorking.

Miriam Dorking, yes.

Bob Ah! (*mysteriously*) Ahh—Dorking. You know about Dorking, do you?

Miriam Well, sort of. Well no, not really, it's just that ...

Bob Ask Dennis. He knows all about Dorking. He knows all about everything.

He "smiles", drinks and moves away behind the drinks bar. Miriam moves quickly out after him

Miriam Yes, but Bob ...

During the above, Ginnie goes into the pavilion

On seeing Ginnie, Miriam stops speaking and goes into the kitchen

*Ginnie moves straight to the bar, where Bob is pouring himself another drink.
She pours herself some water from the jug on the bar*

Ginnie I hope you're pleased.
Bob What've I done now?
Ginnie (*holding up her bottle*) I'm back on the Valium, dearie.
Bob You were never off the Valium, dearie.

Ginnie looks at him pityingly and starts to go into the changing-rooms

Bob Ginnie ...
Ginnie That's you and me finished, you know that, don't you?

Ginnie exits into the changing-rooms

*Bob toasts her with his glass. There is a great deal of activity from the field—
Kevin, Dennis and particularly Roger showing concern—on their feet, shouts
of "Go back go back!" Bob hurries to the door just as the gloom is settling in,
and it is Kevin's turn to panic*

Bob Wass happened, wass happened?
Roger Charles—run out.
Bob He's done it again—he's bloody done it again!

*Dennis alters the board to read: 71 for 5, last man 5. The men applaud the unseen
Charles as he leaves the field. Kevin prepares to go out*

Maggie Kev, come here ...

*Maggie moves to Kevin to plant a kiss on him and hoik up his pants, so that
his entrance to the field is somewhat undignified, fending off his adoring wife.
Maggie sits in the canvas chair and watches play much more attentively now.
As Kevin goes out, she claps loudly*

Kevin exits to the pitch

Roger (*more interested elsewhere*) What's wrong with Alex? Why's he coming
in? (*He stands up*)

Alex enters, pulling off his new batting gloves

What's wrong?
Alex Bloody glove's split.
Bob (*pointing with his glass*) You ran me out, you bugger!
Roger Miriam! Gloves, gloves!
Dennis Here we are, here we are.

Dennis takes a pair to Alex

Alex (*tossing down the other pair*) Where did this cheap rubbish come from?
(*He starts to go, ignoring Bob's following remark*)
Bob That's Dennis' cheap rubbish that is, and you ran me out, you bugger!

Alex goes off to the field

Roger Keep it going, Alex, great stuff—right, who's in next? (*He looks at the book*) Christ, it's me! (*In a panic he scuttles inside, pulling off his large sweater*) Score, score—somebody score. Miriam!

Bob I'll score—don't panic, don't panic ...

Roger scuttles through into the changing-rooms

Bob sits at the score table, with his glass of scotch, and leans down close to focus on the book raising his glasses

Whose is this great big blob? Oh it's you, Dennis, sorry old chap. Still—you're steady, I'll give you that.

Dennis moves inside and goes behind the bar to pour himself a can of beer

Miriam comes out of the kitchen as Ginnie comes out of the changing-rooms

Ginnie The door's jammed.

Miriam Sorry?

Ginnie The ladies' loo, the door's jammed, you can't get in, I had to use the other one.

Miriam I'll tell Roger.

Ginnie Yes, that's right, Miriam: you tell Roger and then he'll tell you and you can fix it. Chop chop.

With a "smile" Ginnie goes outside. Dennis comes out from behind the bar

Miriam (*moving to him*) Dennis—you remember you once said if there was anything I wanted to talk about, I should talk about it to you? Well, there is.

Dennis (*taking her hand*) What's that, my lovely?

Miriam Dorking.

Dennis Dorking.

Miriam *Vis-à-vis*—Roger.

Dennis (*after a moment*) Ah—*Dorking.* (*He changes the subject deliberately clumsily*) I don't understand my wife, you know. New house on a very superior estate, own car—only twenty-two thou' on the clock which can't be bad, can it—plenty of time to pursue her own hobbies—all right, so the kids are gone but they all have to fly the nest sooner or later, don't they? But is she happy—is she?

Miriam You were telling me about Dorking.

Dennis Ah. Well now. Difficult. I mean ...

Suddenly Maggie puts two fingers to her lips and whistles loudly—Kevin having scored his first run. She whistles thus and shouts encouragement—"Lovely goal, Kev!"—and the inappropriate like, throughout. Dennis takes the opportunity of moving outside to the verandah

Roger comes out of the changing-rooms adjusting his box. He turns his back on Miriam as he does so

Miriam Roger ...

Roger What?

She cannot bring herself to say the word

Well, come on then, come on.
Miriam (*blurting it out*) Surrey.
Roger What?
Miriam Chessington Zoo, Leatherhead—Box Hill.
Roger Well?

Miriam funks it completely, and hurries into the kitchen

Roger scowls after her and goes outside

Miriam enters from the kitchen lighting up a king-sized cigarette which she smokes fiercely as she comes out on to the verandah

God I'm tense. (*He revolves his tense neck*)
Ginnie That's because you do too much, Roger. All this, I mean. And virtually single-handed from what I hear.

Miriam puffs her cigarette violently at this

Dennis Fair's fair now: one mustn't forget Miriam.
Ginnie One doesn't forget Miriam: one couldn't forget Miriam.
Roger You're quite right though, Virginia. I was just the same at school. Incredible organizer. I was captain of cricket then as well you know.
Miriam Yes, that's something I've never really understood, darling.
Roger What is?
Miriam Why you've never really—well—improved. I mean—if you were captain then, shouldn't you be a field-marshal or something by now?
Roger Very good Mim, yes, ha-ha. (*He revolves his neck*) God, my neck.
Maggie Would you like a massage?
Roger Do you do that sort of thing?
Maggie Kevin says I'm fantastic.
Roger Oh—well—in that case then—just there.

Roger indicates his neck and shoulders. Maggie moves to sit on the steps and he sits in front of her, so that her legs straddle him. She massages his neck and he totally submits, closing his eyes in almost cat-like pleasure. Miriam stands smoking, studiously watching the game

Miriam.
Miriam Yes, darling?
Roger I hope you're making a note of this.
Ginnie She will be, I know she will be.
Roger Seeing how it's done.
Miriam Yes, I am, darling.
Maggie You've got quite a nice little body in its own way. Nice little plumps.
Miriam Plumps?
Maggie Those things there. (*She indicates his deltoids*)
Miriam Oh—plumps. Yes, hasn't he?
Ginnie Oh God.
Roger I've always been keen on sport you know. I suppose that's why I've kept in trim.

Miriam When we went to Corfu for our honeymoon, he took his cap and his box, just in case there was a game going, didn't you darling?

Maggie What box?

Miriam His box. You know. (*She does a rather inhibited mime showing where his box is*) To protect his thingies.

Maggie Oh—his *box*. (*To Roger*) You would have made someone a lovely baby.

Roger (*referring to the massage*) That's incredible—super.

Maggie I can't have babies.

Roger I'll be your baby.

Maggie Will you really?

Miriam Oh he will, he will.

Maggie Would you let me bath you in front of the fire?

Miriam He would, he would.

Maggie And powder your little bottom and put a nice clean nappie on you?

Miriam He would, he would.

Roger It's true, it's true. (*To prove the point, he stuffs his thumb in his mouth and wiggles his toes*)

Ginnie Oh God.

Maggie There. (*She pats him, indicating he is finished*)

Roger (*getting up*) Fantastic.

Dennis moves towards Maggie, slipping his coat from his shoulders with a leer

Dennis Me next?

Maggie Have you got athlete's foot, Dennis?

Dennis Me? Hardly my love.

Maggie Oh. Only I noticed when you kept touching me earlier on, how damp your hands were. I just wondered if dampness was a general condition of yours.

She smiles at him naïvely. He smiles, but is again aware of being got at

Roger Miriam—make a note to pop down to the college of further education, see if they do physio.

Miriam Yes, darling: do you want me to sign on for physio before or after I've signed on for car maintenance?

Bob Eighty up!

Bob staggers round to change the board

Maggie Have you got children, Virginia?

Ginnie Just the one.

Maggie How old?

Ginnie He'll be thirty-nine next March.

Roger (*sighing happily*) I was just thinking. I haven't seen a butterfly for years. Miriam—what's happened to all the butterflies?

Miriam I don't know, darling. Perhaps they've all gone to Dorking.

Ginnie We saw a butterfly last night, didn't we Bob?

Bob Yes we did, actually.

Ginnie In the garden.

Bob We were having a quiet drink together—just the two of us.

Miriam How nice.

Ginnie He was going to mow the lawn but he tired himself out rolling up his sleeves.

Bob No point in cutting the stuff is there? Only grows again.

Ginnie But then you're bound to get tired, aren't you, darling, it's all that running around you do. (*She moves quickly inside the pavilion*)

Bob Look after the book a minute, will you Dennis old chap old chap?

Bob goes inside after Ginnie who ignores him, keeping her back to him. So he pours himself another scotch

Roger God, I could do with a fag.

Miriam Have one of mine, darling. (*She moves to him, grandly proffers her packet and puffs out a huge cloud of smoke*)

Roger You're smoking.

Miriam Yes, darling.

Roger I didn't know you were smoking.

Miriam Oh, there's a lot you don't know about me, Roger. (*She laughs gaily, taking a huge draw on her cigarette*)

Roger What does that mean?

She blows out smoke and waves a coquettish finger

Miriam Aha!

Roger (*bewildered*) But we gave it up together.

Miriam goes to sit next to Dennis and speaks loudly enough for Roger to hear

Miriam About that drink, Dennis.

Dennis Pardon?

Miriam I can probably manage next Wednesday.

Dennis Err ...

Miriam Super.

Roger whirls round to her, about to demand an explanation, but there is a great roar from the pitch. The men react—the applause being that much larger because the man out is Alex. Roger scuttles around, collecting up bat and gloves, and Dennis changes the board to read: 83 for 6, last man 44

Roger How many do we need?

Dennis Err—fifty-five.

Roger looks defiantly out at the opposition

Roger *Right!*

Roger strides away manfully

Bob He's out is he? 'Bout bloody time.

Alex comes in moodily and tosses down his bat on the way into the changing-rooms

Alex Well, that's it, isn't it?

Bob That's what?

Alex I've gone, so we've got no chance, have we?

Bob Wadda you care? You don't care about the team, all you're concerned about, matey, is missing your lousy fifty.

Alex Well let's face it—I'm the only one capable of making it—aren't I, *matey*?

Alex exits irritably into the changing-rooms

Bob moves to Ginnie. Maggie rises to her feet, shouting, and miming the pulling up of pants

Maggie Kev! Hitch 'em up, hitch 'em up!

Bob sits next to Ginnie

Ginnie She phoned you.

Bob looks up slowly and nods

Liar.

Bob 'Strue. (*He crosses his heart*)

Ginnie Does it ever occur to you she may not want you over there? Does it?

Bob I haven't told you what she wanted yet.

Ginnie I don't want to know. You fool, you stupid fool. (*She starts to move away, then turns*) When are you going to get it into your thick head, you're not married to her any more—you're married to me. And I can't take much more of this, I swear it, Bob, I swear it ... (*She is almost in tears—bitter, frustrated tears*)

He stands, tries to comfort her

Bob Ginnie love ...

Ginnie shakes him off and hurries outside. She snatches up her beach-bag, drags out a handkerchief, and quickly exits round the side of the pavilion

Dennis and Miriam, in particular, notice her distress

Alex comes out of the changing-rooms with a Mars Bar. He tries to ignore Bob

Juss a minute—you ran me out, you bugger.

Alex Oh, don't start that all over again. (*He starts to go, then turns*) You're getting past it, old chap. (*He "smiles"*) The flesh is willing but the brain is weak. (*He steps out on to the verandah*) How we doing? (*Not that he cares but he wants to draw attention to himself*)

Dennis Ah, there you are, Alex—damn rotten show that, you should've had your fifty.

Alex I'm bloody well sick, I can tell you.

Bob (*shouting from inside*) *You* haven't got a brain!

Alex kneels, staring fixedly at the game and chewing on a Mars Bar

Maggie Have you seen your girl-friend?

Alex does not respond

(*To Miriam*) What's his name again?
Miriam Alex.
Maggie Oi—Alex! (*She gives a piercing whistle*)

Alex stares at her

Have you seen your girl-friend?
Alex No—where is she?
Maggie Sitting in your car.
Alex Now look here, she's not fiddling with my switches, is she?
Maggie I think you should go and have a word with her, don't you, chutney?

Alex looks at Dennis as if to say "Hello, what have we got here?", starts to move past Maggie, but stops to point at her fur coat

Alex Is that thing dead?
Maggie I dunno: it's about as lively as you, I should think.
Alex Sweet.

Alex goes off round the corner. Bob comes out, having poured himself another drink

Bob Where is he? (*To Maggie*) He's a solicitor you know. I blame solicitors for everything. Smug bastards. (*Shouting*) I'm gonna complain about you!
Dennis Do the book, will you?
Bob Certainly, Dennis, old sport, certainly.

Bob grins his way to the table as Dennis makes way for him

Dennis Thing about solicitors—they wouldn't have anything to do, would they—if people like you didn't keep giving them so much business.

Dennis "smiles". Bob prods him and does a thumbs-up, you're-dead-right look

Bob (*confidentially*) I say, Dennis—should I need another divorce, can you get it for me wholesale?

Dennis moves nearer Maggie

Dennis I hope she hasn't made any sort of commitment to these people.
Maggie Who?
Dennis My wife. She's been looking at new houses you know and if I'm not there people are liable to take advantage. She's not terribly bright, poor old thing: I understand it's congenital.
Maggie Oh dear: I'm surprised a man of your intelligence ever married her, it must be very depressing for you.
Dennis Ah well, thereby hangs another as they say. Perhaps I might unburden my soul some time?
Maggie Oh yes, I'd like that.

He discreetly pats her bum and moves away. She grimaces: he makes her feel sick

Ginnie enters, having been crying. She wipes her eyes with a handkerchief as she comes, then holds the handkerchief to her nose

Miriam Are you all right, Virginia?

Ginnie Yes, thanks—I think I've got a cold starting. (*Suddenly, angrily at Bob*) You and your rotten cricket!

Maggie Would you like to borrow my coat?

Ginnie (*meaning "thanks"*) Oh—well ...

Maggie takes off the huge fur and gives it to Ginnie, who slips it over her shoulders

Alex enters from round the corner

Alex No, she isn't—where is she, she's got the keys to my car.

Bob (*shouting*) I'm not talking to you! Rotten solicitors.

Maggie I think you should go and look for her, don't you?

Dennis (*generally*) Did I tell you I've got a new car? A BMW.

Ginnie sits on one of the benches. Dennis moves inside the pavilion. Alex looks up and down for Sharon

Ginnie Did you hear that, Bob? Someone has arranged his life so that he can actually keep enough of his money to buy a new car.

Bob Funny thing about me—I've never really had this maudlin interest in other people's success stories.

Ginnie The funny thing about you darling is, you've never really had an interest in *anything.*

Maggie (*to Alex*) Why don't you go and look for her?

Alex You don't like me, do you?

Maggie No.

Alex "smiles", moves off and exits round the corner

Ginnie He loses his enthusiasm so quickly you see—jobs, hobbies, marriages, count ten and he's bored. That isn't to say he doesn't try—he's a very trying man, aren't you, darling?

Miriam (*"lightly"*) We're not starting a little tizzy, are we?

Ginnie Have you ever tried nursing someone with terminal boredom, Miriam?

Bob Marriage should have followed religion into disrepute, that's what I say. (*He nudges Miriam, winks broadly*)

Ginnie We don't all have the perfect marriage, you see, Miriam.

Dennis goes to sit at the piano

Miriam (*still 'pleasantly"*) I've never suggested that my marriage was perfect—far from it.

Ginnie Not *awfully* far from it, Miriam, surely? Just a few miles up the A24.

Dennis begins to play a sad and simple little tune—part of a Galuppi sonata. Miriam moves inside the pavilion

Bob A man can live perfectly happily with a woman without getting married to her. Look at me and my mother. Spotless I was, spotless.

Ginnie It's true: his underclothing was the talk of Willesden.

Miriam moves to the piano and "arranges" herself against the wall

Miriam Am I so very unattractive, Dennis?
Dennis (*stopping playing*) You Mim? Never.
Miriam Do I appear awfully bossy to you? You don't have to tell me, it's not compulsory, you know.
Dennis (*sincerely*) Miriam—you're all *right*.
Miriam I've always been completely faithful to Roger, I want you to know that.
Dennis Yes I'm sure you have.
Miriam One is. By nature.
Dennis One knows that.
Miriam But one can change. One can only stand being called an officer and a gentleman for so long.
Dennis The thing is—I think we should think very carefully about it.
Miriam Very carefully about what?
Dennis About Wednesday. (*He takes her hand and does his sincere bit*) We mustn't rush into anything we won't be able to control. The heart is a strange animal. I know.
Miriam But I've always been able to control *everything*. Don't you see? That's my trouble.
Dennis Let's—you know—think about it.

He holds his sincere look, gives her hand a final pat, and resumes playing the piano. Miriam sinks. Ginnie moves across to Bob, who grins amiably at her and indicates his glass

Bob I've only had two little ones, you know.
Ginnie (*flatly*) You've been divorced for over a year. But still you go round there. Still you pay the rent and mow the lawn and fix the shelves and do whatever else you and your bloody guilt complex think you ought to be doing.
Bob Ah—yes—*but* ... (*He gives her a big thumbs-up and grins*)
Ginnie Oh God, what have I done with my life? Why don't you go back to her? You're there most of the time, anyway.

Dennis stops playing and drifts outside

Maggie Can you hear banging?
Miriam Sorry?
Maggie I thought I could hear someone banging ...

They listen

Yes.
Miriam It's in here.

Miriam goes through into the changing-rooms

There is the sound of a regular and increasingly loud banging

Bob Ninety up!

Dennis changes the board. Bob stands, hand to head dramatically

I am ill, I know I am. In fact I think I'm dying—my whole life keeps flashing in front of me.

Alex enters

Most of it seems to have been spent in a solicitor's office paying their rotten bills.

Alex Now look, I'm not interested in all that bloody nonsense—I've lost the keys to my car.

Dennis moves to Maggie

Bob (*dramatically*) Not—the keys to your *car!*
Dennis Something else, you know. She nags. Nag nag nag, never stops. I can't see you nagging young Kevin.
Maggie I used to but he put a stop to it.
Dennis Oh yes—how?
Maggie I was going on a bit and he said if you don't shut up while I'm doing my pastry I'll put one on you and I didn't shut up so he put one on me. A right uppercut, I think it was. He's got a fantastic right uppercut, my little Kev, you wouldn't think it, would you—comes right up from the floor it does.

Maggie points to the floor and Dennis looks down. Suddenly she mimes a huge uppercut that just misses his chin, and she smiles

Mind you, give him his due, he'd never hit a man.

During the above Miriam returns from the changing-rooms

Miriam She's locked herself in.
Alex Who?
Miriam Sharon.
Alex What d'you mean, locked herself in?
Miriam The lock's stuck. In the ladies' loo. I'm afraid she's having hysterics.
Alex Well—do something medical.
Maggie Like what?
Alex Well I don't know—throw a bucket of water over her or something.
Miriam The *door's* stuck.
Alex Well don't look at me, I'm a lawyer, not a bloody lavatory attendant.
Bob Same thing, old boy, same thing.

Miriam hurries back into the changing-rooms as there is sudden activity from the game

Alex Now look here Wiley, I'm just about sick and tired of your ...
Dennis (*pointing*) Hello—what's happened?
Bob They've laid him out, the dusky devils!

They all look towards the game

Maggie That's my little Kevin!
Dennis Hello, he's coming off.
Maggie (*shouting, waving a fist*) You leave him alone, you—you—racist bully!

Maggie hurries to assist the incoming Kevin

Bob He got hit with a bouncer—right on the bonce. (*He performs an exaggerated mime of the event*)

Maggie returns, assisting the injured Kevin. He is a bit dizzy and is holding his head

Maggie (*shouting back*) He's only little, why don't you pick on someone your own size? (*She helps lay him out on a bench*)
Kevin A drink, a drink—I need a drink.
Maggie Someone get him some water.
Kevin I said a drink, you dozy cow.
Maggie (*to Dennis*) Where d'you put that wine?
Dennis Right!

Dennis goes inside, behind the bar and gets the bottle of white wine and a bottle opener which he puts into the cork

Roger dashes in irritably, waving his bat

Roger Where's bloody Donald?
Bob (*shouting amiably*) Bloody Donald!
Roger What's the score?
Bob (*peering at the book*) Ninety-seven.
Roger Well, put it up, then!
Bob There isn't a seven, can't find the seven.
Roger Look—just keep that board moving—I want to know exactly where we stand!

Roger dashes back to the arena

Kevin I'm cold.
Maggie Can I have my coat back, please? (*She snatches her fur coat from Ginnie's shoulders and throws it over Kevin, covering his head and upper body*)
Kevin Everything's gone black!
Maggie I'll get something for your head.

Maggie hurries inside and exits to the changing-rooms as Miriam comes out and sees Kevin

Miriam What's happened?

Ginnie pulls the coat down to reveal Kevin's head

Ginnie They attacked her little Kevin.
Kevin It was personal, I know it was.
Alex Sue them, old boy.
Bob Typical—bloody typical! (*He moves to the board, alters it to read 98— then takes down the 6—stares—puts up the 8, takes it down, puts up the 6 again*)
Miriam (*to Alex*) I really think you ought to speak to her.
Alex What good will I do?
Bob No bloody good *at all*!

Miriam She says she's embarrassed and she is your—you know—your thingy.

Alex Just tell her to pull herself together and put my keys under the door, all right?

Maggie returns with a damp towel and moves straight outside

Maggie (*to Alex*) Get in there, you great slob!

Alex Now look here ...

Maggie thrusts a clenched fist under his nose

Maggie Piss off before I put one on you!

Alex recoils and mumbles his way inside—"all right—all right"—and into the changing-rooms

Kevin You're quite right, Mag, you'll make a lovely mother.

Dennis moves outside as Maggie sits putting the towel round Kevin's head. Dennis kneels next to them, trying to pull the cork. Maggie snatches the bottle from him, puts it between her legs and yanks out the cork with the one hand then holds the bottle for Kevin to drink as though he were a baby. He sits in the fur coat and towel turban, swigging. Bob is in a right state with the board. The score now reads 988. He stares—takes off the 8 and tosses it over his shoulder—replaces it with a 9—repeats it, staggering, so that the score reads 999. He stares at it

Ginnie He won't let go of her, you see. He won't let go of anything. D'you know, he's still got the bike his father gave him when he passed for the grammar school? Just a heap of rust at the end of the garden, but he won't get rid of it because his dear old working-class dad gave it to him. He's so bloody *guilty*—and what's guilt if it isn't self-indulgence, tell me that? (*She moves to sit, tearfully, on the lounger*)

Roger (*off, shouting*) Keep that bloody board moving!

Bob (*shouting back*) Stuff you! The only reason we're here is so's you can have your rotten game of cricket, you silly little twit! (*He kneels by Ginnie*) All the time I've been going over there—doing things for her—she's been going with another fellah. I said to her, "Why didn't you stop me? Why couldn't he mow the lawn and mend the rotten fence?" And you know what she said? "I didn't want to disappoint you," she said.

Roger dashes in, furious

Roger Miriam!

Miriam Yes, darling?

Roger Who's on the board?

Miriam Err ...

Roger (*pointing*) Get on that board and keep it moving, woman!

Miriam Yes, darling.

Roger stomps off

Miriam hurries to stare at the scorebook

Bob She's getting married. Thass what she wanted to tell me—she's getting married—so she won't be needing me any more—not for money, not for anything.

Ginnie She's getting married?

Bob We're gonna be all right—she won't be needing me any more—and I love you. (*He kisses her gently*)

Miriam Hundred up!

Alex returns from the changing-rooms and comes outside

Alex She's locked herself in the bog.

Kevin We know that.

Alex She says she won't come out until you've all gone, so d'you mind? (*He indicates "clear off"*)

Maggie Well, talk her out.

Alex *Talk* her out?

Kevin Talk her out—like they do in films, only with aeroplanes. (*He puts the bottle to his mouth, his box to his ear*) Control tower to bog, control tower to bog, are you reading me?

Maggie Go on—go and pretend you're Charlton Heston.

Alex If you think I'm standing there, having a conversation through a lavatory door—what am I supposed to talk about? I only met her yesterday ...

Bob rises and moves menacingly towards Alex

Bob Lissen you! Not only did you run me out but you deliberately turned your back on that catch when I was bowling, you coward—and not only that, I lost my family because of the likes of you—bloody solicitors—making money out of other peoples' personal misery. Well I'll tell you this— I may be a lousy husband and a lousy father but I'm a damn good cricketer and no-one—no-one—can say otherwise—all right, mister smart-arse rotten lawyer?

All the time Bob speaks he prods Alex backwards and Alex offers bored "yeah, yeah's." As Bob finishes his speech he clicks fingers in Alex' face and Alex falls backwards into the canvas chair, which tips up throwing his legs in the air and he lies sprawled

Miriam Oh Alex—pull yourself together, there are standards, you know.

Maggie (*pointing towards changing-rooms*) What about *her*?

Alex (*legs flailing*) What about *me*?

Miriam The window ...

Alex What?

Miriam Talk to her through the window.

Alex I can't talk to her through *anything*.

Maggie It's too high.

Miriam Fetch the ladder.

Roger (*off*) Miriam!

Maggie Go on you—fetch the ladder.

Alex I have broken my neck!

Kevin Sue them old boy, sue them.
Maggie Dennis—fetch the ladder.
Dennis Certainly—where is it?
Maggie Miriam, where's the ladder?
Miriam Through the kitchen, on the right.
Maggie (*jerking a thumb*) Through the kitchen, on the right.

Dennis scuttles into the kitchen

Alex I shall sue! I shall sue the bloody lot of you!

Bob advances on him again

Bob Lissen you. I may be a lousy cricketer—but I'm a bloody good husband—
and father—and son—you ask my mother.

Miriam claps the activity on the field

*Bob, misconstruing, bows to her and exits, weaving, to the car-park. Dennis
comes out of the kitchen, staggering under the weight of a pair of steps*

*Maggie goes to Dennis, snatches the steps, and carries them past Miriam with
one hand*

Miriam D'you need some help?
Maggie Thankseversomuch, it's not compulsory.

Maggie exits round to the car-park

*Kevin moves to sit beside Ginnie who slowly begins to sob. He offers her a con-
soling drink from the bottle*

Ginnie She's getting married.
Kevin Oh?
Ginnie I'm so happy.
Kevin Oh.
Ginnie At least—I think I am—I don't know—I think I am ...

She begins to sob freely and Kevin comforts her

Roger stomps in furiously waving his bat

Roger Who is doing the bloody *scoring*?
Miriam I am, Roger.
Roger Well do it, woman, do it! And stop that crying! If you've got anything
to cry about, do it through me, I am the captain! Where's Kevin?
Kevin Here I am and I am very nearly unconscious.
Roger Well don't pass out, I may need you. (*He starts to stomp out again*)
Miriam Roger!
Roger What!
Miriam Tell me about Dorking!
Roger What?
Miriam I said—I am not a machine!

Roger stomps to thrust his face into hers

Roger Then what other excuse have you got?

Roger stomps off out to the game again

Miriam stares after him, and suddenly shouts, near to tears

Miriam I am not a machine! Do you hear me, dearie? I am a fully-qualified and totally-frustrated Pitman's shorthand typist—*and* secretary of the Ivor Novello Appreciation Society!

Miriam storms tearfully inside and exits into the kitchen

Dennis takes up the fallen book and makes an attempt to resume the scoring

Maggie returns with the ladder and drops it on Alex's feet as she passes his chair

Maggie All yours, sunshine.
Dennis I say, careful old love, that's my ladder. (*He goes across to take up the ladder*)

Maggie moves to Kevin

Maggie Fancy a game o' darts?
Kevin I might, I might not.
Maggie Suit yourself.

Maggie goes inside and starts playing darts. There is a great cry of "Howzat!", and Dennis drops the ladder into Alex' lap

Dennis Oh gawd, that's Donald gone ... (*He moves to the scorebook and adjusts the score*)

Sharon bursts out of the changing-rooms

She sees Alex, who is struggling with the ladder, goes to him and starts to flail him with her handbag

Sharon and Alex exit towards the field, she flailing and he trying to defend himself with the ladder. Bob returns from the car-park, beaming all over his face

Bob I say—whose is the new red BMW?
Dennis Not mine, mine is polychromatic silver with a black hide interior.
Bob Not any more it isn't, it's red.
Dennis How can it be red, you drunken idiot?
Bob Because your wife just set fire to it. (*He beams*)

Dennis grins—then his face changes and he sniffs the air and dashes off round the corner with a half-disbelieving, half-horrified cry

Dennis Shirley? Shirley my love?

Bob looks at Kevin and Ginnie, who can scarcely contain their delight

Kevin She didn't.
Bob 'Fraid so.
Ginnie *Never.*

Bob I must say, it's burning beautifully. Muss be all that polychromatic paint.
Maggie Are you serious?
Ginnie Shouldn't someone send for the fire brigade?
Bob It's being done.
Maggie There must be something we can do.

Maggie starts to go to the car-park, but Kevin stops her with a manly air

Kevin *I'll* do it—you'll only hurt yourself.

Kevin exits to the car-park

Maggie looks after him adoringly and rolls up her sleeves

Maggie Am I going to give him a seeing-to when I get him home tonight ...

Maggie exits after Kevin

Bob Keep it going till I get there! Women and solicitors first! (*He puts an arm around Ginnie, kisses her lightly, and guides her towards the car-park*) D'you know what she told me—Shirley—when she was tipping petrol onto his vinyl roof and I was pretending not to notice? He doesn't get things wholesale, he only says he does. He has to pay full price like everyone else. It's his way of making people like him. Sad really. P'raps he thought he wouldn't get a game if he wasn't getting us cheap jockstraps.

There is the sound of activity from the field

I suppose someone ought to be doing the board.
Ginnie (*a great cry to the heavens*) Oh God!

Ginnie and Bob exit, arms around each other, to the car-park. Silence for a moment, then Miriam comes slowly out of the kitchen

She stands, realizes no-one is there, then moves outside, still slowly, and picks up a plate with orange peel on it. She moves around, collects more peel, and puts it on the plate, then stops, looking down at it. She starts to sing quietly, "Some Day My Heart Will Awake", then deliberately tips the peel and plate all over the grass and skips back inside the pavilion, singing more loudly

Roger dashes in

Miriam sings even louder, skipping past him

Roger What the hell's happening? Where is everyone? Miriam!

Suddenly Miriam moves before the board, arms outstretched, pressing her body against it

Miriam Tell me about Dorking!
Roger What?
Miriam Unless you tell me about Dorking, this board remains stationary!
Roger Miriam—*please*—I am playing the definitive captain's innings out there ...
Miriam Yes darling, and it's super.
Roger Well get back on that bloody board!

She snatches the bat from his hands

Miriam I will darling, just as soon as you tell me about Dorking.

He tries to get the bat back, but she holds it like a club

Roger Right! If you remember, you didn't come to Dorking last year because one of the kids went down with the scarlet whatsits ...

Miriam Yes, darling, I remember.

Roger Well, I told you how Piggy Pearson who used to be Fatty Woolacott's best friend at school turned out to be the captain of this Dorking shower we thrashed the pants off ...

Miriam Yes, darling, sort of.

Roger Well you'll remember how I was late home because the fan belt went on the Volvo.

Miriam Yes, darling.

Roger Well it didn't.

Dennis stumbles back from round the corner, hair awry, clothing dishevelled, grabs the hosepipe and turns on the tap

Dennis She's round there laughing at me—Shirley—she's laughing at me ...

Dennis dashes off, dragging the hosepipe

Roger Are you going to get back on that board?

Miriam No!

Roger Right! Piggy's got this divorced sister who took a bit of a shine to me and if you must know, when you thought I was fixing the fan belt, I was indulging in a spot of naughties.

Miriam staggers, shocked, as there is a cry from the pitch to tell Roger to get a move on

Roger (*shouting to the players*) Yes, all right all right all right! (*To Miriam*) Just the once mind, nothing in it of course, and no need to ask you if you understand, of course you do, so will you please get back on that board, we are half a dozen runs away from victory and I must keep track! (*He snatches the bat from her hands*)

Miriam (*dazed*) Keep track of what, darling?

The sky begins to darken

Roger (*pointing the bat*) The board!

Miriam Yes darling—but getting back to that other business—(*advances on him*)—I'm just the teensiest weensiest bit surprised you haven't mentioned it before—bearing in mind that it has always been our solemn agreement should such a happening occur.

He almost thrusts two fingers into her eyes

Roger *Two* reasons—(a) it didn't seem worth mentioning at the time, and (b) when I did get round to telling you, you were planning your bloody menu for next week's match and somehow it didn't seem right to disturb you. All right, okay, fair enough?

She stares at him, then suddenly gives a scream, knocks all the numbers from the scoreboard and hurries past him and into the pavilion

Miriam Good-bye, Roger.
Roger Waddaya mean—good-bye?
Miriam I mean I'm going home, collecting the children and leaving you!
Roger (*with a cry of pain*) Oh my God! Oh my God!

Roger slumps on to a bench and Miriam dashes out again

Miriam I didn't mean it darling, I didn't mean it! (*She sits alongside him, throwing comforting arms around him*)
Roger Mean what?
Miriam About the children.
Roger The children? Are you completely insensitive, woman? Can't you feel it? (*He looks towards the heavens*) It's beginning to rain!

There is a great roll of thunder and the sky darkens. Miriam and Roger sit, side by side, staring dejectedly for a moment

Miriam Well, in that case, darling—I'd better put the kettle on.
Roger (*a broken man*) Oh Miriam ...

She sighs, stands, and moves slowly inside the pavilion

Miriam No, it's all right thankyou. I can manage ...

Miriam moves wearily towards the kitchen, and Roger stares miserably out towards the pitch as—

The CURTAIN *slowly falls*

FURNITURE AND PROPERTY LIST

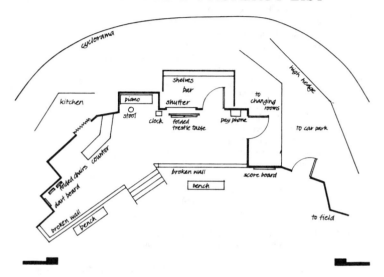

ACT I

On stage: **PAVILION**

Drinks bar with wooden shutter. *On shelves:* assorted drinks, including whisky, bottle of white wine, glasses, jug of water, soda syphon, cork opener, can opener

2 bar stools

Upright piano. *On top:* cricket trophies. *In keyboard:* bar key

Piano stool

Tea counter. *On it:* ashtray. *Under it:* cardboard box of crockery; cardboard sign LADIES' FIRST DOOR ON RIGHT. *Behind it:* rubbish bin

Folded trestle table against wall

Folded chairs, wooden

On walls: clock, pay phone with pencil and note pad, dartboard with darts, notice-board with various notices and spare pins

On changing-room door: hook

OUTSIDE

2 wooden benches. *On one:* bucket of whitewash, marking-up stick, whitewash-splattered wicket-keeping gloves

Upstand water-pipe with hose attached

Cricket scoring board

Small table or shelf for scorer

On verandah and grass: odd pieces of rubbish

Off stage: Team list (**Roger**)
                Folded newspaper (**Roger**)
                2 cardboard boxes of groceries (**Miriam**)
                Tea towel (**Miriam**)
                2 bars of soap, roll of Andrex, aerosol spray (**Miriam**)
                Sports bag (**Dennis**)
                Scruffy cricket bag (**Kevin**)
                Box full of lettuce, cucumbers, etc. (**Miriam**)
                6 crates of beer (**Dennis**)
                Duster (**Miriam**)
                Plastic pot of cutlery and polishing cloth (**Miriam**)
                Packet of Elastoplast (**Dennis**)
                Large tatty team bag with cricket pads, gloves, etc. (**Dennis, Roger**)
                Tablecloth in plastic bag (**Maggie**)
                Cricket bag (**Ginnie**)
                Scorebook (**Miriam**)
                Cricket ball (**Kevin**)
                Leather holdall (**Alex**)
                Alex's cricket whites on hanger under plastic (**Sharon**)
                Several pairs of cricket pads (**Roger**)
                Cricket stumps (**Roger**)
                Cricket bat and ball (**Alex**)
                Large bottle of meths (**Miriam**)
                Sun lounger (**Ginnie**)

Personal: **Roger:** watch, pencil stub, keys, money
                Bob: 2p piece, cigarettes, lighter, watch
                Miriam: handbag
                Dennis: bag of sweets, car keys, handkerchief, cigarettes, lighter
                Maggie: handbag with tissues, folding screwdriver, cigarette roller with
                    papers and tobacco, matches, large spectacles
                Ginnie: dark glasses, large beachbag with paperback novel, bottle of
                    Valium, aerosol spray, handkerchief, lint pad
                Kevin: cigarettes, lighter
                Sharon: large handbag
                Alex: car keys

ACT II

Set: 2 wooden chairs outside for scorer, with scorebook and pencil
                Number plates on scoreboard and scattered on ground
                On ground outside generally: odd plates, cups, pieces of orange peel,
                    jumble of cricket pads, bats, batting gloves
                On counter and table: trays, used plates, cups, saucers, spoons

Off stage: Pads, gloves, bat (**Dennis**)
                Broom (**Miriam**)
                Protective helmet with visor (**Dennis**)
                Packet of king-size cigarettes, matches (**Miriam**)
                Mars Bar (**Alex**)
                Damp towel (**Maggie**)
                Pair of steps (**Dennis**)

Personal: **Miriam:** apron, yellow plastic gloves
Bob: clip-on Polaroid lenses
Maggie: copy of *Socialist Worker*, bag of toffees
Kevin: over-large umpire's coat
Dennis: wallet with business card, handkerchief, 2p piece

LIGHTING PLOT

Property fittings required: nil
Exterior. A cricket pavilion. The same scene throughout

ACT I

To open: General effect of sunny summer early afternoon

No cues

ACT II

To open: General effect of summer afternoon, still sunny but
              about 4 hours later

Cue 1:   **Miriam:** "Keep track of what, darling?"   (Page 73)
            Sky begins to darken

Cue 2:   **Roger:** "It's beginning to rain!"   (Page 74)
            Sky darkens further

EFFECTS PLOT

ACT I

Cue 1:	**Maggie** wipes nose with tissue *Telephone rings*	(Page 14)
Cue 2:	**Miriam:** "Roger ..." *Telephone rings*	(Page 32)

ACT II

Cue 3:	As CURTAIN rises *Sounds of bat on ball, and applause from field*	(Page 37)
Cue 4:	**Bob:** "I *had* to play, didn't I?" *Applause*	(Page 38)
Cue 5:	**Maggie:** "... she needs exercise" *Applause*	(Page 38)
Cue 6:	**Roger:** "Blame him, not me" *Cry of "Howzat?"*	(Page 39)
Cue 7:	**Bob:** "Me?" *Shout and applause*	(Page 41)
Cue 8:	**Bob** exits to bat *Scattered applause*	(Page 42)
Cue 9:	**Kevin** and **Roger** stare as **Bob** faces first ball *Shout of "Howzat?"*	(Page 43)
Cue 10:	**Maggie:** "... little body is trembling, it is" *Applause*	(Page 43)
Cue 11:	**Roger:** "I hate 'em, I hate 'em" *Applause*	(Page 44)
Cue 12:	**Kevin:** "... a giant, she is, fantastic" *Applause*	(Page 46)
Cue 13:	**Roger:** "Come along, then, woman, chop chop" *Telephone rings*	(Page 49)
Cue 14:	**Maggie:** "... that should do the trick" *Burst of activity from field, and applause*	(Page 50)
Cue 15:	**Dennis:** "... to the dear old thing, now could I?" *Cry of "Howzat?"*	(Page 51)
Cue 16:	**Maggie** sits in canvas chair *Shout from the field*	(Page 52)
Cue 17:	**Bob** toasts **Ginnie** after her exit *General noise from the field*	(Page 57)
Cue 18:	**Roger** whirls round on **Miriam** *Roar from the field, and applause*	(Page 61)

MADE AND PRINTED IN GREAT BRITAIN BY
LATIMER TREND & COMPANY LTD PLYMOUTH

MADE IN ENGLAND